WORLD ORDER

LONDON : HUMPHREY MILFORD

OXFORD UNIVERSITY PRESS

WORLD ORDER
IN HISTORICAL PERSPECTIVE

BY

HANS KOHN

*Sydenham Clark Parsons Professor of History
in Smith College*

CAMBRIDGE, MASSACHUSETTS

HARVARD UNIVERSITY PRESS

1942

PRINTED AT THE HARVARD UNIVERSITY PRINTING OFFICE

CAMBRIDGE, MASSACHUSETTS, U.S.A.

TO THOSE
WHO STROVE AND FOUGHT
FOR THE DIGNITY OF THE HUMAN BEING
FOR THE ONENESS OF THE HUMAN KIND

Εἰ δὲ Σύρος, τί τὸ θαῦμα; μίαν, ξένε, πατρίδα κόσμον
ναίομεν· ἕν θνατοὺς πάντας ἔτικτε Χάος.

MELEAGER OF GADARA (*floruit* 90 B.C.)
Oxford Book of Greek Verse, No. 586

Who knows not that there is a mutual bond of amity
and brotherhood between man and man over all the
world, neither is it the English Sea that can sever us
from that duty and relation.

MILTON, *The Tenure of Kings and Magistrates*

PREFACE

THIS VOLUME concludes a series of books of which the first was written in 1936, when the Second World War started; this, the fourth, appears in 1942, when the United States, through joint Japanese and German action, has been brought to realize the nature of the war. In this as in the First World War, Germany and Japan are bidding for world leadership, backed by superior military force and by a readiness for its unrestrained use. This war, however, is fundamentally different: the Germans and Japanese have joined their efforts for world hegemony — a development unpredicted in 1914 — and they profess the same radical rejection of the basic conceptions of civilization — an attitude which would have seemed fantastic a quarter of a century ago. This very fact of an unprecedented situation has confused our minds and dimmed our vision. But even the unforeseen has its roots in history and may be clarified by an analysis of its background and of the ideas dominating and expressing its fundamental attitudes. By such an analysis alone can be gained the understanding and the perspective needed as guides towards the solution of the world crisis, of which the Second World War is at the same time a product, a symptom, and an aggravating factor.

The one hundred and fifty years from the second half of the eighteenth century to the beginning of the twentieth have been on the whole the happiest period of human history. They have given an unprecedented scope to the development of rational order and individual liberty. But towards the end of the nineteenth century, still in the midst of unparalleled progress,—progress in the fields of science and mechanical invention, but even more in the refinement of our attitudes toward our fellow-men and in the growth of social consciousness — ideas and trends in fundamental contradiction to the liberalism of the age began to reassert themselves. My little book *Force or Reason* tried to analyze these ideas and trends — the "cult of force," the "dethronement of reason," and the result of imperialism. These phenomena set the general background out of which the challenge of the two last decades arose. That this challenge was not met by an adequate response was explained in *Revolutions and Dictatorships* by the failure of most people to see that "beneath all the surface clashes it is not a conflict" for a new balance of power, or between rival imperialisms, or for the revision of a peace treaty, "but one of the great decisive struggles of human history. We have almost forgotten that all great struggles of history were fundamentally struggles between moral and spiritual forces, struggles of ideas. At present we find the moral foundations of our world, as developed under the influence of Christianity and of rational humanism, questioned and savagely attacked by a new philosophy of man and of his place in history. Japan, Italy, and Germany are leading, in a concerted effort, the struggle on behalf of this new philosophy. It is a revolution of anarchy and egotism against the established order of moral and intellectual

values, values only very imperfectly realized
in the life of modern civilization but acknowledged as the regulative principle, guide, and
restraining discipline. It is a battle being
waged with a totalitarian world-embracing
victory in mind. War has become in our days
as indivisible as peace."

While *Force or Reason* dealt with the
origins of the crisis, *Revolutions and Dictator-*
ships attempted to analyze the crisis itself, in
its manifestations from 1917 to 1939. It tried
to clarify the much-used concepts of dictatorship, revolution, democracy, and peace,
and to distinguish between their various
meanings and implications. More important
than similarities of form are differences in
substance and ultimate goal. The book was
written in the winter after the Pact of Munich, when the crisis had already become
apparent, but still was misjudged by all those
who did not understand that they were challenged and that on their response their survival depended. Amid the still widespread
hope for evasion, it has become clear that
"the crisis can be overcome only by the re-

assertion of the moral values of that civilization which is threatened by the crisis, a reassertion which presupposes clear recognition of the new situation in which they have to stand the test. It is an entirely new and deeply frightening certitude that there is no longer any escape in isolation. It is no longer possible in a terrifying world to withdraw like Candide and to cultivate our own garden. The totalitarian crisis burdens everyone, everywhere, with an unprecedented responsibility; it is easily understood that the peoples refuse to shoulder it. But as great as the fear and the danger is the hope; for the first time the possibility dawns of establishing peace and liberty, not for ourselves, but for mankind. We cannot save ourselves first; in the totalitarian crisis we all stand or fall together."

Not by Arms Alone appeared in the fall of 1940, after France's disintegration and betrayal, but also after Britain's refusal to submit had broken the supposed "wave of the future." Reality had proven that "the danger to democracy arose out of failure to comprehend the issues that were involved. The final realization of their danger shocked the democracies into action, sometimes when it was very late, always when it was later than they thought; but it did not in every case arouse them to a full awareness of the truth that a world revolution is now in progress."

This war and the coming peace cannot be won without a supreme exertion of armed power, nor can they be won by arms alone. The survival of civilization depends upon the dauntless resolution and unflinching fortitude of its defenders, and these in turn presuppose the historical perspective of the issues involved and a courageous vision of the future order. In 1941, ten years after Japanese aggression in Manchuria, five years after Italy's conquest of Ethiopia, Germany's militarization of the Rhineland and the combined fascist attack upon Spain, all the great powers of this earth found themselves involved in a life-and-death struggle. But more than their freedom and survival were at stake. The dignity of the individual and his place in society; nationalism as a form of political, cultural, and economic organization; the changing and conflicting concept of empire and imperialism; the essence of civilization itself, all these fundamental aspects of human life depend upon the outcome of this war. Never has mankind faced a world crisis comparable to the present one. Its unprecedented challenge can be met only by an unprecedented response, the establishment of a world order based upon liberty and equality. Historical perspective can show us that the four fundamental concepts of democracy, nationalism, empire, and civilization point in their own development and inner logic to the possibility and necessity of a world order in response to the present world crisis. With the forcing of the United States into the war, Japan and Germany have staked the future of the whole world upon the issue of this final struggle. There is no third possibility. In an infinitely deeper and more encompassing way than he could have understood them then, Abraham Lincoln's words addressed to the Congress of the United States on December 1, 1862, are true today: "The dogmas of the quiet past are inadequate to the stormy present. The occasion is piled high with difficulty, and we must rise with the occasion. As our case is new, so we must think anew and act anew. We must disenthrall ourselves, and then we shall save our country. Fellow citizens, we cannot escape history. . . . We shall nobly save or meanly lose the last, best hope of earth."

                                        H. K.

Northampton, Mass.
January, 1942

ACKNOWLEDGMENTS

The first chapter, in a slightly different form, first appeared in *Whose Revolution?* edited by Irving De Witt Talmadge (New York: Howell, Soskin, 1941), the second in the *American Political Science Review*, December 1939. They are reprinted here with the permission of the publishers, to whom I wish to express my thanks. I wish also to express my appreciation of Miss Olga Zhivkovitch's conscientious coöperation in the preparation of this volume.

CONTENTS

DEMOCRACY

THE WAY OF MAN

Without stopping to qualify the averment, the Old World has had the poems of myths, fictions, feudalism, conquest, caste, dynastic wars, and splendid exceptional characters and affairs, which have been great; but the New World needs the poems of realities and science and of the democratic average and basic equality, which shall be greater. In the center of all, and object of all, stands the Human Being, towards whose heroic and spiritual evolution poems and everything directly or indirectly tend, Old World or New.

WALT WHITMAN, "A Backward Glance o'er Travel'd Roads"

Chapter One

DEMOCRACY

THE WAY OF MAN

T HE present war has been rightly regarded as a decisive battle between a totalitarian form of government and the liberal way of life developed through the intellectual and social revolutions of the seventeenth and eighteenth centuries. Such a struggle is nothing new; the last two hundred years were full of it. What distinguishes this crisis from all preceding ones is on the one hand its universal scope, and on the other hand its decisive character.

In the second quarter of the twentieth century all movements have assumed a new and universal character because of the tremendous changes in locomotion and communication. The struggle between democracy and reaction in Europe one hundred years ago was strictly limited to that continent; today the same struggle draws all continents into its orbit. Totalitarianism claims universality and universal application by its own definition, whether it be the totalitarianism of a religion or the totalitarianism of a political philosophy such as communism or fascism. Unless stopped, its dynamism necessarily drives it towards realization on a world-wide scale. The present world-wide conflict between totalitarianism and democracy is of a decisive nature because the countries involved are not selected by historical accident or by secondary considerations. The countries involved are potentially strong enough to wage the struggle decisively for the whole world, and they are the very nations that have developed in their cultural and social traditions the prototypes of the totalitarian and the democratic ways of life.

Though all totalitarianism claims universality, only the German form of totalitarianism has the power and the aggressive extremism to make good its claim. Russian communism, like the religious totalitarianisms, has lost the spirit of aggressive extremism and has never developed the military and economic power for large-scale aggression. It is not communism but the fear of communism that represents a threat to the survival of democracy. Nor is Italian fascism a real danger to democracy on a world-wide scale. Italian fascism, after eighteen years of preparation, broke down under the very minor strain of the wars against Greece and Egypt. The secondary fascisms draw their universal importance from Germany's support, and depend upon it. Only Germany, through its unique military tradition, the high efficiency of its industrial equipment, and the discipline and intelligence of its population, can make good the totalitarian claim to universality.

Of all the democracies, the United States is, because of its geographic position, its numerous population, its large resources, and its supreme industrial equipment, the only power to match Germany. Thus the struggle of totalitarianism against democracy reduces itself ultimately to one between Germany and the United States. There is no doubt that the Germans have known this. It does not matter, for the existence of the struggle, whether the Americans knew it or willed it. The less they knew it the greater were Germany's chances of victory.

But it is not only a question of power which reduces the conflict ultimately to one between Germany and the United States. In the years since the first World War the world has come to be so much of a unit, the earth has been shrinking so much in its extent, that an organized world becomes more and more necessary. The leadership in this organization can be exercised only by Berlin or Washington. In comparison, Moscow, London, and Tokyo, not to speak of Rome or Paris or Madrid, are secondary centers of power. German totalitarianism and American democracy tend to represent, in the most outspoken form, the totalitarian and the democratic trends.

The American Revolution at the end of the eighteenth century and the German Revolution of the second third of the twentieth century form, not only in their programs, but even more in their consequences, the most definite expressions of two opposite and irreconcilable trends of political, social, and intellectual development. All the great currents of the Western liberal development of the seventeenth and eighteenth centuries were able to ripen to fruition under the especially favorable circumstances of the English colonies in North America and in the wake of their revolutionary movement. Here, more than anywhere else, emerged the Western man; not as a race, because he was a mixture of all races, but as a social and intellectual type, professing a deep faith in man and his potentialities, and trying to build a civilization on the basis of rationalism, optimism, and individualism. The American society more than any other is a product of the eighteenth century, of the faith in freedom and in ultimate harmony; a typical middle-class society with its ultimately pacifist ideal. German totalitarianism, which has its roots deep in the past of German development since the Renaissance and the Reformation, is a complete and uncompromising rejection of the Western man and his society, of the optimism, rationalism, and individualism of the eighteenth century.

2

The end of the eighteenth century marked a sharper dividing line between two stages of human development than any other short span in history. Its incomparable strength was founded on its universal message, on the promise to establish a new order in which all men and all peoples would participate equally — a new era which would assure liberty and justice for all and bring forth hidden well-springs of a higher morality to build the city of man in the whole world. True, in the cross currents of historical realization these generous impulses were soon inextricably intertwined with all kinds of old and recent vested interests, of traditional and of untried emotions, of desires and appetites aroused by unprecedented opportunities, and of fears and anxieties born of the insecurity of changing times and unknown destinies; but the main trend was unmistakable. It aroused new

hopes and new joy in being human in the
hearts of the peoples throughout Western
Europe, and spread from there at the beginning of the nineteenth century to the countries of Central and Southern Europe. But
the Europeans of the time themselves knew
that the European soil was not the right nurs-
ery for the growth of the new order: the
forces of the past were too strongly entrenched. More propitious seemed the soil
where men lived near the healing forces of
Nature, in whose fundamental goodness the
eighteenth century so strongly believed —
where conditions were relatively simple, and
where few of the vested interests and cor-
ruptions of a traditional and aristocratic
civilization hindered the growth of the spon-
taneous goodness of man. No wonder that
Europeans looked longingly toward the vast
spaces of North America, where they saw the
possibility of establishing a society without
kings or nobles, a society founded upon the
philosophy of the century. Though the
Americans had come from Europe, they
seemed to be changed men, as if the air of

America were filled with liberty and were able to transform men's minds and hearts. The new order of rational enlightenment and of the equality of all individuals seemed to have better chances in a new land than in the old countries where the foundations of the old order, based on authoritarianism, superstition, and inequality, survived.

In this new world all the liberal influences of the seventeenth and eighteenth centuries seemed gathered under unique circumstances. From England came the English tradition of constitutional liberty and common law, helped by the young and experimental character of the settlements so remote from European society. The impulse of the Puritan Revolution remained much more alive in New England than in the mother country, where the Restoration had infinitely greater influence. Efforts at establishing religious and class forms of domination never fully succeeded; new waves of immigrants, coming mostly from the lower classes and bringing various religious affiliations with them, prevented the rigid stabilization of such a domination for any protracted period. Characteristically, those Puritans who returned from the colonies to England in the middle of the seventeenth century carried back with them a resolute optimism for social betterment and supported the left wing of the Puritan revolution. One of them, Hugh Peters, said in a sermon preached to Parliament in England on April 2, 1645: "I have lived in a Countrey, where seven years I never saw beggar nor heard an oath nor looked upon a drunkard; why should there be beggars in *your* Israel where there is so much work to do?" [1]

The early settlers of New England were sharply divided in the interpretation of the "holy experiments in government." One school, under men like Cotton, tended toward institutional theocracy; the other, under men like Hooker and Williams, tended toward prophetic religion. Both, however, regarded the settlements as a new beginning, with immense potentialities for the improvement of the race. By the beginning of the eighteenth century this feeling had crystallized into the conviction that the New World settlements represented the most perfect fruit and at the same time the noblest possibilities of English development. As Jonathan Edwards put it, Providence intended America to be "the glorious renovator of the world"; and John Wise, Pastor of Ipswich, Massachusetts, maintained in 1717 that "the end of all good government is to cultivate humanity, and promote the happiness of all, and the good of every man in all his rights, his life, liberty, estate, honor, etc., without injury or abuse to any." [2]

The American Revolution was not foreshadowed by any state of oppression or of misery, by any feeling of bitter disloyalty or despair. On the contrary, the colonists were the least oppressed of all people on earth. They were not only infinitely freer than all people on the European continent, they were even freer than Englishmen in Great Britain. The American colonists revolted not because they were oppressed but because they were free, and their freedom carried the promise of still greater freedom, one impossible of realization in the more settled and static conditions of old society, but beckoning as a possibility in the new continent. Mother country and the colony grew from the same roots — the Magna Carta and common law, Parliamentary institutions and local self-government, the Puritan and the Glorious revolutions, Milton and Locke. The American Revolution was a consummation of English liberalism. The demands of the colonists found as warm defenders in Great Britain as at home, not only among "radicals" but also among the highest dignitaries of the Crown and the Law, men like Charles Pratt, Earl of Camden, who called the British Constitution one "whose foundation and center is liberty, which sends liberty to every subject" within "its ample circumference."

But the American Revolution appeared not only as a consummation and fruition of the English revolutions of the seventeenth century, but also as the product and the consummation of the new natural-rights doctrine of the eighteenth century and of the

French political thinkers, with their new emphasis on the interpretation of liberty not as a historical and constitutional right but as a rational and universal attribute. "I always consider the settlement of America with reverence and wonder," John Adams wrote in 1765, "as the opening of a grand scene and design in Providence for the illumination of the ignorant, and the emancipation of the slavish part of mankind all over the earth." [3]

It is noteworthy that the "philosophy" of the American Revolution was not supplied by one of the colonists but by an Englishman who had landed only a few months before in America. Thomas Paine's *Common Sense* was written by a citizen of the world who saw in the American Revolution a struggle for the birth of a new freedom on universal principles. It was the "religion of humanity" which vibrated in every page of the clarion call to independence and which helped the American Whigs to gain a new consciousness of their actions and aims. Through this interpretation the American Revolution formed a vanguard of mankind, building a society on entirely new foundations — the human rights of the eighteenth century. In the Declaration of Independence, eighteenth-century political theory found its first application in the world of reality.

By the end of the Revolution, the American colonies had emancipated themselves from the past so completely that they did not regard common descent or a common root in the past as a foundation of their community. In 1784 Benjamin Franklin, in his "Information to Those Who Would Remove to America," stressed the fact that "birth in Europe has indeed its value; but it is a commodity that cannot be carried to a worse market than that of America, where people do not inquire concerning a stranger, What is he? but What can he do?" [4] He stressed the mutual tolerance and peaceful coöperation of many sects and creeds in America; yet this diversity and tolerance in religion, elsewhere unheard of in that period, was matched by the diversity and tolerance of the racial strains in the colonies. As far back as 1782 a keen observer like Crèvecoeur

could point out the emergence of a new man
in the United States and the astonishing
variety of the racial elements mingling in
the melting pot: "He is an American who,
leaving behind him all his ancient prejudices
and manners, wrests new ones from the new
mode of life he has embraced, the new government he obeys, and the new rank he
holds. He becomes an American by being
received in the broad lap of our great alma
mater. Here individuals of all nations are
melted in a new race of man, whose labors
and posterity will one day cause great
changes in the world." [5] Here a nation
emerged founded on general and rational
principles, not looking to the past but constituted wholly by consciousness of a common present and a common future. "The
Gothic idea that we will look backwards
instead of forwards for the improvement of
the human mind, and to recur to the annals
of our ancestors for what is most perfect in
government, in religion and in learning, is
worthy of those bigots in religion and government by whom it has been recommended,

and whose purposes it would answer. But
it is not an idea which this country will endure." Thus Thomas Jefferson wrote to Doc-
tor Priestley in 1800. And in even more
succinct form, he summed it up when he
wrote in 1816, "I like the dreams of the
future better than the history of the past." [6]

3

The American nation which arose in the
American Revolution was not bound together
by ties of blood or of the past. Nor was it a
nation rooted in the soil, as the European
nations were. American nationalism has
been primarily the embodiment of an idea,
which, though geographically and historically located in the United States, was a universal idea, the most vital and enduring
legacy of the eighteenth century. An example was here set to mankind, not only in
the republican form of government but also
in its federative character, combining the far-
reaching independence of historical separate
communities with the existence of a strong
central authority for common concerns. The

Constitution and the Bill of Rights have remained the unshakable foundation of the new nation. They have drawn their strength not from their legal character but from the ideas which they express. In spite of their imperfections they have withstood the test of time better than any other constitution on earth, for during the past one hundred and fifty years all other nations everywhere have changed their constitutions repeatedly. The American constitutional laws have lasted because the idea for which they stand was so intimately welded with the existence of the American nation that without the idea there would have been no American nation.

Among the realities of national life the image which a nation forms of itself and in which it mirrors itself is one of the most important. Though the everyday reality, in many ways, does not correspond to the image and falls far short of its ideal perfection — sometimes even contradicts it in the countless and conflicting trends of the complex actuality — nevertheless, this image, woven of elements of reality, tradition, imagination, and aspiration, is one of the most influential agents in forming the national character. It helps to mold national life; if it does not always act in a positive direction, it acts at least as a constant brake. "It is still certain," wrote Thomas Jefferson to Joseph Priestley, "that though written constitutions may be violated in moments of passion or delusion, yet they furnish a text to which those who are watchful may again rally and recall the people; they fix, too, for the people the principles of their political creed." [7] Nations not rooted for many centuries in a circumscribed soil, or nourished by the belief in common descent, live even more by the force of the national idea. The territory of the United States was not circumscribed; in spite of Noah Webster's efforts, the country never even developed a language of its own; Negroes, Jews, German Lutherans, and Latin Catholics participated in the Revolutionary War and fought for the nascent American nation; it was the national idea alone which could serve as a foundation.

It is interesting to note that the image

which Europeans formed about the new American nation at the end of the eighteenth century was not different from the Americans' idea of themselves. America appeared as a symbol of liberty and "natural" virtue, a land in whose vast open spaces the natural order could become creative, unhampered by the traditions and superstitions of past ages. This interpretation abroad reacted upon Americans' own conception, the more so because it gladly conceded the leadership of America on humanity's road to the future. For the first time a nation had arisen on the basis of these truths held "to be self-evident, that all men are endowed by their creator with certain unalienable rights, that among these are life, liberty, and the pursuit of happiness" — truths which the nation could not give up without destroying its own foundation. Through all the many public sermons, articles, and poems, with their empty bombast and rhetorical unctuosity and their tribute paid to the tastes of the times, through all the political struggles and economic maneuvers of petty men and greedy leaders, the American ideal lived — disfigured and sometimes obliterated, but still struggling for its realization.

The new nation, born in the American Revolution, was based upon the faith that it was different from other nations, different not in representing a peculiar and unique development of human history but rather in being the first to realize a general trend of human development towards a more rational order, more individual liberty, and greater equality. American nationalism is thus not a movement of romantic protest against the equalitarian and rational attitude of eight-eenth-century Western Europe, as German and Russian nationalism have been in many of their leading representatives, but is the very consummation of this Western attitude. It is not a voice crying out of the depths of the dark past, but proudly a product of the enlightened present setting its face resolutely toward the future. Noah Webster praised the American system of civil government be-cause it had been "framed in the most en-lightened period of the world. All other

systems of civil polity have been begun in
the rude times of ignorance and savage
ferocity; fabricated at the voice of necessity,
without science and without experience.
America, just beginning to exist in an advanced period of human improvement, has
the science and experience of all nations to
direct her in forming a plan of government." [8]

America, it was believed, had realized
what the leading thinkers of the French and
English Enlightenment had outlined as the
future of humanity; she came to regard herself as the trustee of the universal blessings
of liberty and equality for Europe and for
mankind. Soon the French Revolution
seemed to follow in the wake of the American Revolution; even one of the proudest
creations of 1793, universal military service
in the citizens' army, had been foreshadowed
by the patriot armies of the American Revolution. The French Revolution in its turn
acted upon the American public mind, and a
new wave of democratic enthusiasm swept
America in the 'nineties. Though it had received its strength and its public appeal

from the French Revolution, nevertheless, it sprang from the very foundations of the American Revolution. The French Revolution had acted everywhere in Europe as an agency vitalizing the peoples to liberty; but in the United States the resurgence of ardor and faith in liberty, equality, and fraternity was not a passing phenomenon quickly to be submerged by the victorious counter-revolution. While in Europe despotism seemed to triumph, while even in France the new liberties waned, in the United States the second revolution strengthened the existing foundations of Americanism and made them impregnable.

A fervent friend of the French Revolution, Joel Barlow, could proudly establish the unique position of the United States: "In the United States of America the science of liberty is universally understood, felt, and practiced, as much by the simple as by the wise, the weak and the strong. Their deep-rooted and inveterate habit of thinking is, that all men are equal in their rights, that it is impossible to make them otherwise; and this

being their undisturbed belief, they have no
conception how any man in his senses can
entertain any other. This point once settled,
everything is settled. Many operations, which
in Europe have been considered incredible
tales or dangerous experiments, are but the
infallible consequences of this great principle." [9] The fight against oppression and
inequality, for individual liberty and social
justice, the faith in the common man and his
perfectibility — this common task and duty
of mankind seemed to Jefferson and to his
contemporaries more possible of realization
in America than anywhere else. It was this
faith of the American people in itself and in
its mission which made it a nation. The
American form of government was "a standing monument and example for the aim and
imitation of the people of other countries." [10]

This multi-racial nation, whose farming
population was rooted in the mobility of the
frontier instead of in the immobility of the
soil, was integrated around allegiance to
the American idea, an idea to which every
one could be assimilated for the very reason

that it was a universal idea. It was a nationalism theoretically without any exclusiveness.
Jefferson wished to keep the doors of America wide open, "to consecrate a sanctuary for
those whom the misrule of Europe may compel to seek happiness in other climes. This
refuge once known will produce reaction on
the happiness even of those who remain
there, by warning their task-masters that
when the evils of Egyptian oppression become heavier than those of the abandonment
of country, another Canaan is open where
their subjects will be received as brothers,
and secured against like oppressions by a
participation in the right of self-government." The shore of the new world had been
a land of promise for the early settlers; it
would be so for all newcomers as long as
need existed. And finally the need would
cease: all other countries would accept the
blessings of liberty and equality for which
the American form of government stood.

Ten days before he died, in the last letter
which is preserved, Jefferson reiterated his
faith in the American mission which had

animated him when he had written the Declaration of Independence half a century before. "May it be to the world what I believe it will be (to some parts sooner, to others later, but finally to all), the signal of arousing men to burst the chains under which monkish ignorance and superstition had persuaded them to bind themselves, and to assume the blessings and security of self-government." [11] The same inclusive and liberal idea even molded American imperialism. In "A Poem on the Happiness of America," which David Humphreys addressed to the patriot armies of the Revolution, he contrasted past empires built upon conquest with the new rising empire erected on "freedom's base" and dedicated to "humanity's extended cause."

Throughout its subsequent history the original attitude of American nationalism lived on as one of the determining forces of the young nation's destiny. Its manifest destiny may have demanded the annexation of Canada or Cuba so often clamored for in the nineteenth century, but beneath the apparent surface deep restraining impulses were active. "The American expansionists' nationalism was so little exclusive that it offered refuge to all the devotees of freedom in a world elsewhere threatened with a rising deluge of despotism." [12] All new lands were open to newcomers on equal terms under the protection of that fundamental recognition of the "great and equal rights of human nature" which was a foundation of American nationalism as the legacy of the eighteenth century. America's expansion was also an expansion of democracy. America has visualized her own national birth as a step in the struggle for the liberty of the individual and the happiness of the whole human race; though she may allow the consciousness of herself — and her conscience — to become obscured in certain parts or at certain times, nevertheless she cannot give it up entirely without undermining the foundations of her existence.

The American nation has not been determined by the "natural" factors of blood and soil, nor by the common memories of a long

history. Traditions of the past and regard
for ancient events have always tended to
separate nations; the dead weight of memories of long ago has frustrated efforts at a
rational new beginning. Americans could
unite men of different pasts because, on the
basis of rationalism and individualism, they
rejected the ties of the past. "Happily, for
America, happily, I trust for the whole human
race they pursued a new and more noble
course. They accomplished a revolution
which has no parallel in the annals of human
society. They reared the fabrics of governments which have no model on the face of
the globe." Thus wrote James Madison,[13]
knowing that though the American form of
government was unprecedented and at that
time unique it had its roots in the rational
thought of mankind and would, therefore,
influence, and be imitated by, other peoples.
A new chapter of world history had started
with the American Revolution, and its influence was to spread not only to Europe but
also to the then still undiscovered lands of
the Far East.

4

The American Revolution created the American nation. The German Revolution of 1933 did not create the German nation. Though it is impossible to think of Americanism outside the eighteenth-century foundations of liberty and equality, it is not only possible but entirely legitimate to think of a Germanism outside, and even opposed to, the forms of life produced by the Revolution of 1933. The German Revolution of 1933 has been a profound and far-reaching revolution, transforming and remolding the entire political, social, and intellectual order. It is a radical revolution, going deeply into the roots of all human relations and ways of life and trying to reform them in an entirely different spirit, with their roots implanted in an entirely different soil. This does not mean that the German Revolution represents, as the revolutions of the last three centuries did, progress on the road towards more human liberty and equality. The German Revolution does not establish a new order, but reëstablishes and strengthens the foundations of the old order, the only order which it recognizes as order — the order of authority and inequality. But it is no longer, so to speak, the naïve old order which existed before the three revolutionary centuries. Nor can it be compared to the conservative reaction of the nineteenth century, which kept itself on the defensive and fighting a rearguard action. It is an infinitely more conscious and more aggressive revival of authoritarianism and inequality than the old order has ever known.

The German Revolution goes even beyond the old order in its revival of primitive warrior spirit. The eighteenth and the nineteenth centuries, the bourgeois centuries as they are contemptuously called by the adherents of the "new order," cherished faith in a coming period of lasting peace. It was expressed by Washington when he wrote to Lafayette in 1786: "As the member of an infant empire, as a philanthropist by character, and (if I may be allowed the expression) as a citizen of the great republic of humanity at large, I cannot help turning my attention sometimes to this subject. I would be understood to mean, I cannot avoid reflecting with pleasure on the probable influence, that commerce may hereafter have on human manners and society in general. On these occasions I consider how mankind may be connected like one great family in fraternal ties. I indulge a fond, perhaps an enthusiastic idea, that, as the world is evidently much less barbarous than it has been, its melioration must still be progressive; that nations are becoming more humanized in their policy, that the subject of ambition and causes for hostility are daily diminishing; and, in fine, that the period is not very remote, when the benefits of a liberal and free commerce will pretty generally succeed to the devastation and horrors of war." [14] Washington's hopes were shared and variously expressed by John Bright and Tennyson, Saint Simon and Mazzini, Victor Hugo and Jaurès. Today the sense of moderation, of compromise, of humanitarianism, of live and let live which the nineteenth century came to regard as a civilized attitude is being ridiculed as mediocre and unexciting, and its place is taken by a new aesthetic delight in "heroism," in combat, in the ecstasies of war and violence. Peaceful life is replaced by the tension of permanent mobilization, violence becomes the normal method of government, and power a self-sufficient goal.[15]

This recrudescence of an old order and of old ideals is nothing peculiarly German. Many men of all nations share it today, but nowhere has it been thought through with such methodical earnestness and metaphysical depth, nowhere has it found the same powerful instruments of realization, and nowhere has it found such a propitious soil for its growth as in Germany. As the American Revolution was the product of the whole intellectual climate of the time and of the thoughts of many men in many countries, so the German Revolution is borne by currents to which movements and men in non-German countries have contributed much. But in the same way as the American Revolution was the consummation of the whole liberal trend, so the German Revolution may be regarded as the consummation of the whole counter-revolutionary movement against the human progress of the last three centuries. As the American was the foremost democratic revolution, a climax and an inspiration, so the German Revolution has become the foremost fascist revolution — an extreme and a model.

This is not to say that the German Revolution of 1933 was a necessary outcome of the preceding intellectual and social development of Germany. Like the history of every old and great nation, German history abounds in many and contradictory currents. The fascist Revolution of 1933 carried Germany not by any historical necessity, but as a result of many historical accidents, of mistakes made by its adversaries, of intrigues, and of personalities. The most prominent representatives of German civilization and thought were in no way the forerunners of National Socialism and cannot be claimed by it, even by the widest stretch of propagandist imagination. It is noteworthy that the greatest and as yet unparalleled blossoming of the German spirit occurred in the years between 1770 and 1830, in the period of German political weakness and humiliation. At that time Germany abounded in so many creative spirits in the field of poetry and *belles lettres*, of philosophy and music, that there are few periods in history which equal and none which surpass it. It is equally noteworthy that after Germany established her political hegemony in Europe and later aspired to a similar position in the world, German intellectual life showed a definite weakening of its creative powers compared with the period a century before. The Second and the Third German Reich have nothing to show in the field of philosophy and music, of *belles lettres* or poetry, that can compare with the great classical period of Germanism.

Its leading minds were all representative of a truly humanitarian, individualistic, and universalist attitude; above all Goethe in his mature years, Kant, and Beethoven. The three greatest Germans never doubted that duties towards mankind and the moral law

take absolute precedence over duties towards
the fatherland. The German classical writers
saw men's goal in the perfection of the individual; with all their patriotism, they were
primarily humanitarian and cosmopolitan.
Politically "the ideal of all German classical
writers was a peaceful small state which
seeks its glory exclusively in the arts and
sciences." [16] Wieland praised in 1780 the
existing weak constitution of the moribund
First Reich because it seemed to him to assure best the individual liberty of the Germans. The multitude of existing small states
made it possible for the German subject of a
despotic prince to escape to a neighboring
territory and to choose among the large variety of German princes and political entities
that which seemed most conducive to the
unhampered development of his individual
faculties. Wieland was convinced that "as
long as we [the Germans] will preserve it
[the status of Germany at the time] no great
civilized people in the world will enjoy a
higher degree of human and civic liberty and
will be more secure against political and ec-

clesiastical subjugation and serfdom than the Germans." [17]

Even after nationalism had in the nineteenth century become a dominant tendency in German life, the liberal forces seeking to create a German nation in accordance with the principles of liberty and equality were by no means inconsiderable. It was a historical accident which determined even the course of Prussian development. Had Crown Prince Frederick succeeded his father in 1862, and had Bismarck not become prime minister of Prussia, the unification of Germany could have been accomplished in the spirit of 1848 and with a strengthening of the parliamentary foundations of German political life. The longevity of William I and the premature death of Frederick III sealed a development which in no way can be regarded as inevitable. To deny claims that National Socialism is the only genuine form of German civilization it is sufficient to point out the strictly democratic character of the German-Swiss cantons — undoubtedly Germanic in their origin — and the fact, on the

other hand, that the leading National Socialists and most of their doctrines came from
those Austrian and Prussian frontier lands of
German colonization where the inhabitants
are of the most mixed descent.

Nevertheless, fascism found in Germany a
more fruitful soil than anywhere else. Under
fascism we understand the total and uncompromising rejection of the great Western
revolutions of the seventeenth and eighteenth
centuries, of the spirit of 1688, of 1776, and
of 1789.[18] Fascism implies the denial of individual liberty, of human equality, and of
the desirability of a rational peaceful order.
It glorifies war and warriors, hierarchy and
authority, discipline and obedience. It ele-
vates the distinctive character of each nation,
as opposed to others, to an absolute; it regards this nation and its interests as a first
and foremost consideration and as the only
standard of what is good and true. It therefore rejects all absolute standards of ethics
and law, and thereby the oneness of the human spirit and all intercourse based on reciprocity. It develops a complete cynicism in

relation to moral values, and an ecstasy of action in itself, devoid of any ethical content, except for the intoxication with the group spirit and with devotion to the group. As fascism believes in the immutable status of man, in his being determined by unchangeable biological factors, it denies the perfectibility of men, it reduces man and society to the level of nature. Fascism, an attitude of mind and an interpretation of man, is everywhere represented by individuals and groups — in Italy and Greece, in Great Britain and in the United States, among Jews and among Arabs, in Brazil and in China. As a movement of the twentieth century — a century in which mankind is growing towards a unity unknown in any previous period of history — it is necessarily universal. But of all countries and people Germany offered the best soil for the growth of fascism in its most uncompromising form, and this by no means as a result of the defeat in the First World War, and certainly not as a result of the peace treaty of Versailles, but rather as a consequence of social and political realities and of intellectual attitudes reaching far more deeply into the past and into the texture of the German mind and of German national life.

5

Four different roots of German contemporary totalitarianism are easily discernible: the Prussian tradition, the romantic tradition, the racial theory, and the revaluation of all values to which Friedrich Nietzsche gave the first forceful expression. The kernel of nineteenth-century Prussia, where the Prussian tradition — the spirit of Potsdam — originated and grew, are the lands east of the Elbe — Brandenburg, Pomerania, and eastern Prussia. These lands, which were still inhabited in the thirteenth century by Slavs, were subjugated by German warriors and settlers in whom the mental attitude of colonial times has continued to exist, the feeling of superiority of a master race over a native and passive population. The Hohenzollern princes forged different lands without any organic unity, without common historical traditions, into a new state — a state with very few economic resources, great poverty of soil, and extremely long and almost indefensible frontiers unprotected by any natural barriers. It was the immense will power of the great Prussian kings, especially Frederick William I and Frederick II, which succeeded against all obstacles of nature in creating on the plains of northeastern Germany a powerful state which soon could take its place among the great powers.

They were able to do it by complete devotion to the ideal of a powerful state, by the concentration of all economic, moral, and intellectual resources of the whole population upon one aim, the creation of a powerful army as the center and the life force of the state. It is well known that Mirabeau declared that while other states possessed armies, in Prussia the army possessed the state. In spite of its poverty and its lack of organic growth, the Prussian state developed an army always ready to strike at its enemies unawares, and to strike its deadliest blow. This miracle of will power was made possible by a truly Spartan spirit of devotion to patriotic duty and military virtue, by extreme rational efficiency, frugality, precision, and discipline. In Prussia the army was not only an instrument of policy, it became the ideal way of existence for the whole community, the model of all political and private life. In the nineteenth century, Otto von Bismarck and Albert von Roon made the Prussian army the instrument of the so-called unification of Germany, which was in reality an aggrandizement of Prussia by the direct or indirect inclusion of other German lands under Prussian control.

It is important to understand that in Prussia there did not develop, as in Western Europe, a society independent from the state and critical of the state. The state, as in Sparta, was not only the center of all social and political life, but also the regulating principle of all ethical life and of all moral aspirations. The Germany created by Bismarck "has left the realization of all ethical wants to the state or, to express it in a better way, has expected it in the highest sense from the state." [19]

Bismarck was not a German nationalist. Nor had he any understanding of what present-day German nationalism calls *folk*. He did not serve the German national movement, it served him. Though he was a Christian, he never allowed his religious conceptions to influence or to limit his policy, which was entirely devoted to one aim, the power of Prussia. "His religion meant, in his conception of the state, no more than it had meant in that of Frederick the Great. It had to serve the state, and Bismarck's whole intellectual development is a liberation from the Christian conception of the state. Bismarck would have never said that the state is a moral concept. Such a formula would have appeared to him as an inadmissible limitation of his political methods and aims." [20] This militarism of the Prussian monarchy and this integration of all ethical life in the state and its justification by the state separated the Prussian concept of the state from that of the Western world.

More fundamentally opposed to Western liberalism than the Prussian idea of the state,

however, was German romanticism. In it, as
with Russian nationalism in its Slavophil
tendencies, German nationalism asserted itself against the westernization of Germany
in the wake of the French Revolution and
the influences emanating from liberal and
parliamentary England. The meaning of
romanticism in Germany was different from
its meaning in the Western countries. There
it remained a mode of artistic expression in
literature, while in Germany it became a
Weltanschauung, a philosophic creed, applied to and explaining history, political
theory, law, and the totality of social life
and development. Romanticism continued
in Germany the work begun by the German
humanists of the Renaissance period, who for
justification of Germany's universal claim
to world domination and world leadership
looked to the past, when German tribes had
overrun and subjugated the Roman Empire
and the then known world. The humanists
had identified the Germans of their own day
with those about whom Tacitus had written
his *Germania*, which had just been redis-

covered, and saw in Arminius, who unified
the German tribes for a decisive victory over
Rome, the model German hero.[21] Now romanticism, when it felt Germany's original
inheritance threatened by the intellectual
developments and influences of Western
liberalism at the beginning of the nineteenth
century, took up the fight against Western
enlightenment, against rationalism, against
the spirit of the Western revolutions, with
their emphasis upon individual liberty and
human equality. It regarded the rationalism,
optimism, and individualism of the West as
something hollow and superficial, and liked
to oppose to its clarity the dark profundity
of the German soul. Its eyes were not turned
towards the future, a future common to all
humanity; they were fascinated by the past,
a past which was peculiar to each people.
Instead of the common they stressed the
peculiar; they rejected the concept of equality which gives no superiority to the supposedly exceptional. They rejected the notion
of any common universal law equally binding upon all men and races; and for them

the superior man — and perhaps one day the superior race — was a law unto himself. The concept of the super man and of the super race, which rejects the rational as well as the religious concept of man, dawned upon the horizon of German romanticism.[22]

It was fully developed by the two greatest German thinkers and artists of the second half of the nineteenth century, Richard Wagner and Friedrich Nietzsche. Both were thinkers, artists, and prophets at the same time. Wagner became the first German proponent of note of the racial theory which his son-in-law, Houston Stewart Chamberlain, expounded in *The Foundations of the Nineteenth Century*. The meaning of Germanism changed; while folkdom (*Volkstum*) had been for Herder a purely cultural concept, it became for Richard Wagner a racial concept; he saw the future of Germany in a regeneration of racial consciousness. He directed the attention of the German people to the myths of gods and heroes of a dim prehistoric past; through him they were raised to the dignity of an inspiring example for the twentieth century. The chthonic forces of blood and soil, of hoary and prerational antiquity, were glorified as the determining forces of a history in which man was not capable of any free spiritual growth and perfection and, therefore, fatality alone reigned. The myths which were to express the sense of life and history had no relation to any objective standards of truth, they were measured according to their effectiveness to inspire the will.

Four years after Richard Wagner's death, a German sociologist, Ferdinand Tönnies, published a book, *Gemeinschaft und Gesellschaft* ("Community and Society"), which became fundamental for German social science. It contrasted two ideal types of societal organization. Community saw totality and wholeness in the group, of which the individual was only part. It was formed by unconscious factors, by the deep dark forces of instinct. It was irrational in its origins and in its ties, deeply embedded in the forces of nature, growing organically. It was characteristic of primitive, and to a lesser extent of feudal, times. Society, on the other hand, was characteristic of modern bourgeois civilization. It saw wholeness and totality in the individual, who was prior to the group, which is viewed as a sociological concept owing its origin to rational motives and clear insight into individual interests. Though Tönnies showed some nostalgic longing for the Community, he understood that Society was the mark of high civilization and of a higher morality, that it demanded a respect for truth and law and their universality, a sense of reciprocity and of contractual fidelity, unknown in the more primitive forms. But German social science soon contrasted the "organic depth" of Community, regarded as peculiarly German (though the Russian Slavophiles claimed it as peculiarly Russian), with the "mechanic superficiality" of Society, regarded as characteristic of Western bourgeois society. This contrast was often expressed as that between *Kultur* and civilization. By a daring step one could then doubt the value of civilization and of civilized life at all and oppose to it the primeval forces of nature — a nature not fundamentally good and tending toward harmony as in the eighteenth-century concept, but beyond good and evil, the scene of permanent and meaningless strife and struggle.

This revaluation of all values was the work of Friedrich Nietzsche, undoubtedly one of the leading and most fascinating figures of the latter nineteenth century. Uncannily sensitive, he heralded the still imperceptible approach of a new barbarism. A solitary prophet, with a critical mind of unprecedented sharpness and a burning vision of unprecedented daring, he was typically German in his complete disregard of social and political reality and in his total absorption in pure and irresponsible thought. This lonely philosopher in a vacuum exhibited an audacity of exploration which makes his work one of the most memorable feasts of the spirit; he pushed his thoughts to the limit where the abyss yawns in which he finally lost himself — a tightrope walker over the dark worlds of the subhuman and the titanic, in which the human is irretrievably lost. He

represented an extreme case of the complete
break between the world of thought and the
world of reality, which characterized so much
of German intellectual life; he had no feeling
of responsibility for the consequences of his
thought once it was brought down from his
lofty and unreachable mountain peaks to the
lowlands of common humanity which he
despised.[23]

Relentlessly he unmasked all the shames
and compromises of civilization, all the weaknesses and pettiness of man. Ethics which
had dominated Western life from the time
of Socrates and of the Hebrew prophets —
ethics which found a fundamentally similar
expression in Buddhism, in the Stoa, and in
Christianity — he rejected contemptuously as
a Jewish-Christian invention for the protection of the weak and the dispossession of the
strong. He wished to destroy all the accepted
ethical values, because with their stress upon
equality and humanity, upon pity and charity, they undermined Life. For the new man
for whom he longed, he wrote new tables of
law, the laws of "Life" and "Nature," with

the supreme command to live a strong life, to assert the will to power and domination with good conscience, even if it implies the extermination or the degradation of everything weaker or less vigorous. No goal remains but success in the unending and ever recurrent struggle for self-assertion and power. Success determines truth and goodness. Life is war, and the strong races are the elemental and wholesome forces of triumphant life, which does not care for the musty concepts of ethical goodness or truth.

"For war trains men to be free. What in sooth is freedom? To grow more indifferent to hardship, to severity, to privation, and even to life itself. To be ready to sacrifice men for one's cause, one's self included. Freedom denotes that the virile instincts which rejoice in war and in victory prevail over other instincts; for instance, over the instincts of happiness. The man who has won his freedom, and how much more so the spirit that has won its freedom, tramples ruthlessly upon that contemptible kind of comfort which tea-grocers, Christians, cows, women, Englishmen and other democrats worship in their dreams. The free man is a warrior." [24] And of the strong aristocratic races in which his heart delighted Nietzsche said glowingly: "They revert to the innocence of the beast of prey conscience, like jubilant monsters, who perhaps come from a ghastly bout of murder, arson, rape, and torture, with bravado and a moral equanimity as though merely some wild student's prank had been played, perfectly convinced that the poets have now an ample theme to sing and celebrate. It is impossible not to recognise at the core of all these aristocratic races the beast of prey; the magnificent blonde brute, avidly rampant for spoil and victory. . . . This audacity of aristocratic races, mad, absurd, and spasmodic as may be its expression, the incalculable and fantastic nature of their enterprises, their nonchalance and contempt for safety, body, life, and comfort, their awful joy and intense delight in all the ecstasies of victory and cruelty. . . ." [25]

Nietzsche's foremost disciple was Oswald

Spengler, who in his prediction of the coming age of Caesarism, in his opposition of the power of blood to that of gold, and in his identification of Prussianism with true Socialism, became one of the most important ideological forerunners of National Socialism. He lived long enough to witness what he considered the disfigured realization of his philosophy and to turn away in disgust from the realities of National Socialism, but he had drunk fully from the intoxicating wine of Nietzscheanism, as later interpreted by National Socialism, when he asked: "If I call a man a beast of prey, whom do I offend — man or beast? For the great beasts of prey are noble creatures of the most perfect type and without the hypocritical human morality born of weakness." More than ten years later, in his last work, he wrote jubilantly in the same vein of a world in which fascism had started its triumphal march: "The age-old barbarism which for centuries lay bound and hidden under the severe discipline of a high culture is again awakening, that warlike healthy joy in one's own strength, which despises the age of rationalistic thought and literature, that unbroken instinct of a strong race which wishes to live otherwise than under the pressure of a mass of books and bookish ideas." [26]

Spengler saw the terrifying vision of the new order as it begins to emerge from National Socialist victories; a world in which the multitudes of subjugated peoples will be reduced almost to the level of animals — disarmed, peaceful, and patiently toiling rural serfs, bearing without hope and without revolt the yoke of proud, armed bands of conquerors. In this *pax Germanica* the lethargic masses, dumb and helpless, will resemble Markham's "Man with the Hoe," whose face shows the "emptiness of the ages": "on his back the burden of the world, a thing that grieves not and that never hopes, stolid and stunned, a brother to the ox." Civilization will be dead; primitive times will have returned. How opposed in every line is this future to Walt Whitman's vision: "And it is from such materials — from the democracy with its manly heart and its lion strength, spurning the ligatures wherewith drivellers would bind it — that we are to expect the great Future of this Western world! a scope involving such unparalleled human happiness and national freedom, to such unnumbered myriads, that the heart of a true *man* leaps with a mighty joy only to think of it! God works out his greatest results by such means; and while each popinjay priest of the mummery of the past is babbling his alarm, the youthful Genius of the people passes swiftly over era after era of change and improvement, and races of human beings erewhile down in gloom or bondage rise gradually toward that majestic development which the good God doubtless loves to witness." [27]

6

National Socialism represents the effective blending and vulgarization of these four trends — Prussianism, Romanticism, racialism, and Nietzscheanism — for consumption in an age of masses and industrial technique. All the inner and deep contradictions of the four trends are smoothed over by the emphasis upon German racial mission, according to which the lowliest German is, by the "iron logic of nature," unalterably superior to any member of other races. In the strict hierarchy of races, on which alone a permanent world order can be built, the German race and German thought must lead and must be unconditionally obeyed. German world conquest and totalitarian world revolution become two sides of the same process; their fusion gives uncomparable élan and power to both. An immense confidence that they will be able to mold the world according to their image elates German National Socialist youth. Filled with a fanatical faith, they see only the alternative of world dominion or ruin, *Weltmacht* or *Untergang*. They know that they live in a unique time, a *Weltenwende* or *Zeitenwende*, when what must appear to the outside world as almost unimaginable and unbelievably fantastic can become reality, if willed with wholehearted determination and a brutal will to power, not shrinking before any terror or horror.[28]

Es zittern die morschen Knochen der Welt vor dem
  grossen Krieg.
Wir haben den Schrecken gebrochen; für uns wars ein
  grosser Sieg.
Wir werden weiter marschieren, wenn alles in Scherben
  fällt,
Denn heute gehört uns Deutschland und morgen die
  ganze Welt.

On the road to the goal two great obstacles
present themselves: in the political field the
resources and the will to independence of
the United States; in the ideological field
democracy's love of liberty and individual
dignity. Again, as in the case of Germany
and authoritarianism, the two forces opposed
to German world domination and to the totalitarian world revolution fuse. As a result
of its history and of the present situation the
United States becomes the shield of world
democracy as Germany has become the spear
of world totalitarianism. The ultimate and
decisive adversary of National Socialist Germany is not Great Britain or Russia, though
these must be subjugated and controlled too;
it is the United States.

While German humanists and Romanticists
tried to freeze the world into the forms of

legendary concepts of the Germany in the time of Tacitus or of the Middle Ages, National Socialism reaches even beyond that past to pre-historic times as the decisive mold of future mankind. It is the most audacious counter-revolution ever undertaken, not only against the last three revolutionary centuries, but against the whole development from Socrates and the Hebrew prophets to the present. This most resolute denial of progress does not appear in the form of a conservative counter-revolution, but in that of an aggressive revaluation, with a goal as unlimited as will itself. Reason and the inventions and discoveries of the human mind are put into the service of this will and its relentless drive of force. The second third of the twentieth century, perhaps the most decisive period in world history, witnesses the clash of "two revolutions." National Socialism is the counter-revolution in a revolutionary form. Democracy has been and is the revolution, but it has lost its revolutionary form and inspiration. It must regain its imagination and vision, it must learn again to put will and force into the service of reason. The good, old, simple words, liberty, truth, justice, must again impose their full meaning upon men's life and actions. The revolutionary forces of ethical and human progress which have stagnated in complacency, cynicism, egotism, and irresponsibility can rise to a new clarity under the fire of the counter-revolution. A European philosopher who knows fascism most intimately has pointed out that the apparent decadence of liberty in our time is a strange sort of decadence in that "it is illumined by no flash of a new ideal that is to replace the old, in that no new order is put forward to replace the order that is being attacked. The liberal ideal is a moral ideal, expressing an aspiration towards a better humanity and a higher civilization. The new ideal that is to triumph should present itself with promise of a richer, deeper humanity. Now the one alternative to freedom that is being practically suggested in our day cannot be regarded as offering any such promise. It is the alternative of violence, and violence, whether of race or country, or proletariat, can have no status as morality. Violence contains within itself none of those energies that enhance civilized human living."

Violence or authority is arid, avoiding all critically tested arguments and discussions; it is empty as an ideal of spiritual life. Freedom and equality have been the greatest forces in history to animate men in their strife for a more moral life, for a more human civilization. There is nothing to take their place. The National Socialist faith: world dominion or ruin, can be tested by the liberal faith: freedom or moral death. But here again the philosopher utters a warning with a word that illumines the whole world crisis of our days: "No people will be truly free till all peoples are free." [29]

NATIONALISM

THE WAY OF SOCIETY

The master-key, I suggest, is the conception of the unity of mankind. Most of the evils and frustrations and disappointments from which we are suffering arise from our blindness to this cardinal principle of solidarity and interdependence. It is not the least of the duties of a historian to survey events *sub specie perennitatis*, to see life steadily and see it whole, to visualize the forest as well as the trees.

G. P. GOOCH, *The Unity of Civilization*, Presidential Address to the Ethical Union of London, 1933

Chapter Two

NATIONALISM

THE WAY OF SOCIETY

Nationalism as we understand it is no older than the second half of the eighteenth century. Its first great manifestation was the French Revolution, which gave the new movement an increased dynamic force. Nationalism had become manifest, however, almost simultaneously in a number of widely separated European countries. Its time in the evolution of mankind had arrived, and although the French Revolution was one of the most powerful factors in its intensification and spread, it did not mark the date of its birth.

Like all historical movements, nationalism has its roots deep in the past. The conditions which made its emergence possible had matured for centuries before they converged at its formation. These political, economic, and intellectual developments took a long time for their growth, and proceeded in the various European countries at different pace. It is impossible to grade them according to their importance or to make one dependent upon the other. All are closely interconnected, each reacting upon the other; and although their growth can be traced separately, their effects and consequences cannot be separated otherwise than in the analysis of the scholar; in life, they are indissolubly intertwined.

Nationalism is inconceivable without the ideas of popular sovereignty having preceded — without a complete revision of the position of ruler and ruled, of classes and castes. The aspect of the universe and of society had to be secularized with the help of a new natural science and of natural law as understood by Grotius and Locke. The traditionalism of economic life had to be broken by the rise of the third estate, which was to turn the attention away from the royal courts and their civilization to the life, language, and arts of the people. This new class found itself less bound by tradition than the nobility or clergy; it represented a new force striving for new things; it was ready to break with the past, flaunting tradition, in its opinions even more than it did in reality. In its rise, it claimed to represent not only a new class and its interests, but the whole people. Where the third estate became powerful in the eighteenth century, as in Great Britain, in France, and in the United States, nationalism found its expression predominantly, but never exclusively, in political and economic changes. Where, on the contrary, the third estate was still weak and only in a budding stage in the eighteenth and at the beginning of the nineteenth century, as in Germany, in Italy, and among the Slavonic peoples, nationalism found its expression predominantly in the cultural field. Among these peoples, at the beginning it was not so much the nation-state as the *Volksgeist* and its manifestations in literature and folk-lore, in the mother tongue and in history, which became the center of the attention of national-

ism. But with the growing strength of the
third estate, with the political and cultural
awakening of the masses in the course of the
nineteenth century, this cultural nationalism
soon turned into desire for the formation of
a nation-state.

The growth of nationalism is the process
of integration of the masses of the people
into a common political form. Nationalism
therefore presupposes the existence, in fact
or as an ideal, of a centralized form of government over a distinct and large territory.
This form was created by the absolute monarchs, who were the pacemakers of modern
nationalism; the French Revolution inherited
and continued the centralizing tendencies of
the kings, but at the same time it filled the
central organization with a new spirit and
gave it a power of cohesion unknown before.
Nationalism is unthinkable before the emergence of the modern state in the period from
the sixteenth to the eighteenth centuries. Nationalism accepted this form, but changed it
by animating it with a new feeling of life and
with a new religious fervor.

For its composite texture, nationalism used

in its growth some of the oldest and most primitive feelings of man, which throughout history we find as important factors in the formation of social groups. There is a natural tendency in man — and by "natural tendency" we mean a tendency which, having been produced by social circumstances since time practically immemorial, appears to us as natural — to love his birthplace or the place of his childhood sojourn, its surroundings, its climate, the contours of hills and valleys, of rivers and trees. We are all subject to the immense power of habitude, and even if in a later stage of development we are attracted by the unknown and by change, we delight to come back and be at rest in the reassuring sight of the familiar. Man has an easily understandable preference for his own language as the only one which he thoroughly understands and in which he feels at home. He prefers native customs and native food to alien ones, which appear to him unintelligible and undigestible. Should he travel, he will return to his chair and his table with a feeling of relaxation and will be elated by the joy of finding himself again at home, away from the strain of a sojourn in foreign lands and contact with foreign peoples.

Small wonder that he will take pride in his native characteristics, and that he will easily believe in their superiority! As they are the only ones in which civilized people like himself can apparently feel at home, are they not the only ones fit for human beings? On the other hand, contact with alien men and alien customs, which appear to him strange, unfamiliar, and therefore threatening, will arouse in him a feeling of distrust of everything foreign. This feeling of strangeness will again develop in him sentiments of superiority, and sometimes even of open hostility. The more primitive men are, the stronger will be their distrust of strangers and therefore the greater the intensity of their group feeling. Rudyard Kipling, in his poem "The Stranger," gives forceful expression to the general feeling.

> The Stranger within my gates,
>   He may be true or kind,
> But he does not talk my talk —
>   I cannot feel his mind.

I see the face and the eyes and the mouth,
   But not the soul behind.

The men of my own stock   *common descent*
   They may do ill or well,
But they tell the lies I am wonted to,
   They are used to the lies I tell.
We do not need interpreters
   When we go to buy or sell.

The Stranger within my gates,
   He may be evil or good,
But I cannot tell what powers control —
   What reasons sway his mood;
Nor when the Gods of his far-off land *territory*
   May repossess his blood.

These feelings have always existed. They do not form nationalism; they correspond to certain facts — territory, language, common descent — which we also find in nationalism. But here they are entirely transformed, charged with new and different emotions, and embedded in a broader context. They are the natural elements out of which nationalism is formed; but nationalism is not a natural phenomenon, not a product of "eternal" or "natural" laws; it is a product of the growth of social and intellectual factors at a certain stage of history. Some feeling of nationality, it may be said, existed before the

birth of modern nationalism — a feeling varying in strength and in frequency from time
to time; at some epochs almost completely
extinguished, at others more or less clearly
discernible. But it was largely unconscious
and inarticulate. It did not influence the
thought and actions of men in a deep and
all-pervading way. It found a clear expression only occasionally in individuals, and in
groups only at times of stress or provocation.
It did not permanently or in the long run
determine their aims or actions. It was no
purposeful will welding together all the individuals into a unity of emotions, thoughts,
and actions.

Before the age of nationalism, the masses
very rarely became conscious of the fact that
the same language was spoken over a large
territory. In fact, it was not the same language; the several dialects existed side by
side, sometimes incomprehensible to the man
of a neighboring province. The spoken language was accepted as a natural fact. It was
in no way regarded as a political or cultural
factor, still less as an object of political or

cultural struggle. During the Middle Ages, people deduced from the Bible that as mankind was one it should have one common language, and that the diversity of languages was the result of the sinfulness of man and God's punishment at the time of the building of the Tower of Babel. Consciousness of language was aroused only at times of expeditions and travel or in frontier districts. There, the alien character of the group speaking the alien language was felt, and many names of what we today call national groups derive from the fact that they were first recognized as different groups by those of alien tongue. Some of these national groups even received their names from outside, because they were felt to be a distinct group by an outsider sooner than by a member of the group. The Greek word *barbaros*, which means "strange" or "foreign," and in consequence "rude" and "ignorant," probably has its source in the idea of stammering or inability to speak in a comprehensible way — a word akin to the Sanskrit expression *barbara*, which meant stammering or non-Aryan.

The Slavs called the Germans with whom they came into contact *niemci,* which means the "mutes" — people who cannot make themselves understood. A man speaking an incomprehensible tongue seemed outside the pale of civilization. But language was accepted by the Slavs and by other peoples as a natural fact, not as a cultural inheritance. The language in which the treasures of civilization were inherited and transferred — in medieval Europe as well as in Islam, in India as well as in China — was generally not the language spoken by the people. It was a learned language accessible only to the educated class. Even if it was not a language of different origin from the vernacular, it was generally very different from the spoken language, and on account of its many purely literary, classical associations, was understood by only a small minority.

Before nationalism, language was very rarely stressed as a fact on which the prestige and power of a group depended. Alien languages remained until very recent centuries the languages used by official bodies, in the scholarly world, or among the upper classes. To mention only one fact which stands for a large number: the Breton estates, which were very jealous of their independence, nevertheless spoke French, and in the Act of Union for the Defense of the Liberties of Brittany of 1719 the Breton spokesmen did not mention language grievances. The translations of the Bible in Protestant countries were not undertaken from any motives of nationalism, but purely for the spreading of the true religion. Queen Elizabeth had the Bible and the Prayer Book translated into Welsh, and divine service held in Welsh, to liberate the Welsh from the "ignorance of popery." With the growth of nationalism in the following centuries, still dominated by religion but already harboring the seeds of the new growth, the translations of the Bible certainly were effective in arousing national feeling and in giving a new importance to the national languages, which through the spread of popular education and through the wider use of the printing press, became more and more an element of growing cultural importance. At the same time, the language became uniform, obliterating the vernacular dialects or pushing them into the background, and covering a broader territory as its undisputed domain.

This larger territory became an object of love to its inhabitants only as a result of a long and difficult process. Again this love of the homeland, which is regarded as the heart of patriotism, is not a "natural" phenomenon but an artificial product of historical and intellectual development. The homeland which a man "naturally" loves is his native village or valley or city, a small territory well known in all its concrete details, abounding in personal memories, and in which his life is generally lived throughout its whole span. The whole territory inhabited by what we should consider today as a nationality, a territory frequently distinguished by great diversity of landscape and climate, was practically unknown to the average man, and could become known only by instruction or travel, which before the age of nationalism were limited to a very small minority. Voltaire, who lived before this age, pointed out that "plus cette patrie devient grande, moins on l'aime, car l'amour partagé s'affaiblit. Il est impossible d'aimer tendrement une famille trop nombreuse qu'on connait à peine."

Nationalism is not, as some scholars under the influence of Aristotle suggest,[1] a harmonious natural growth qualitatively identical with love for family and home. It is frequently assumed that man loves in widening circles — his family, his village, his tribe or clan, the nation, and finally humanity and the supreme good. But love of home and family is a concrete feeling, accessible to everyone in daily experience. Nationalism, and in an even higher degree cosmopolitanism, is a highly complex and originally an abstract feeling. It gains the emotional warmth of concreteness only through the effects of an historical development which, by means of education, economic interdependence, and corresponding political and social institutions, brings about the integration of the masses and their identification with a body far too great for any concrete experience. Nationalism — our identification with the life and aspirations of uncounted millions whom we shall never know, with a territory which we shall never visit in its entirety — is qualitatively different from the love of family or of home surroundings. It is qualitatively akin to the love of humanity or of the whole earth. Both belong to what Nietzsche, in *Thus Spoke Zarathustra*, called *Fernstenliebe*, and which he distinguished from the *Nächstenliebe*.[2]

Life in a common territory, subject to the same influences of nature and, to an important although lesser degree, to the same influences of history and legal systems, produces certain common attitudes and traits which are often called national character. We find in the literature of all peoples throughout history frequent characterizations of national groups such as the Gauls or the Greeks, the Germans or the English. Some of these traits seem to persist for a long time, and are mentioned by observers in different centuries. Other traits seem to change under the influence of historical developments.

There are known instances where what was considered at a certain time the most essential character trait of a nation changed after a few decades. In the beginning of the eighteenth century, the English were considered a nation most inclined to revolution and to change, whereas the French were considered a most stable and stolid nation. In the first half of the eighteenth century, Voltaire could voice the general consensus about the English: "The French are of the opinion, that the government of this island is more tempestuous than the sea which surrounds it, which indeed is true." One hundred years later, quite the opposite opinion about the English and about the French was generally held. The English were then, and are even today, considered (and consider themselves) a stolid nation, proud in their disinclination to revolution; while the French were considered a people easily given to and delighting in revolutionary upheavals.

A similar change was produced in opinion about the Germans. One hundred years ago, they were thought a most impractical people,

fit for metaphysics and music and poetry but
unfit for modern industry and business. They
were then the object of a loving admiration
and of a somewhat condescending benevolence on the part of the more practical, and
therefore more powerful, peoples. One hundred years later, the Germans were pro-
ducing very few, if any, metaphysicians,
musicians, or poets of renown, but on the
other hand had become most successful and
practical adepts in modern industry and
business. The attitude towards them changed
correspondingly. The Mongols under Gen-
ghis Khan were warriors famous for their
belligerent character, and brought all Asia
and half of Europe under their yoke. In the
sixteenth century, through the adoption of
Lamaist Buddhism, their old spirit was completely broken and they were turned into
peaceful and pious men. Under the influence
of the Soviet government and its revolutionary propaganda, however, the wild instincts
of the race have been reawakened; and a
new and different consciousness has started
to animate the Mongol people and to break
their religious inhibitions.

The judgments of observers concerning the character of national groups are colored to a varying degree by the political exigencies of the situation or the sentimental attitudes of the author. It seems extremely doubtful whether any judgment about a permanent national character of a people has any scientific value. Between the extremes which may be illustrated by a statement of John Morley that "in the literature of any people we perceive under all contrasts of form produced by variable social influences the one national character from first to last," and the opposite by J. M. Robertson that "the nation considered as a continuous and personalized organism is in large measure a metaphysical dream," we may accept the position of Sir Francis Galton that "different aspects of the multifarious character of man respond to different calls from without, so that the same individual, and much more the same race, may behave very differently at different epochs." Men and men's character are extremely complex; the more so, the less primitive the man is. This holds true even more of a highly complex group like a nation. An

immense diversity of individuals goes into
making up a nation, and during the life-span
of a nation the most diverse influences are
exercised upon it, molding and transforming
it. For growth and change are the laws under
which all historical phenomena fall.

2

Nationalism is first and foremost a state of
mind, an act of consciousness, which since
the French Revolution is becoming more and
more common to mankind. The mental life
of man is as much dominated by an ego-
consciousness as it is by a group-consciousness. Both are complex states of mind at
which we arrive through experiences of dif-
ferentiation and opposition, of the ego and
the surrounding world, of the we-group and
those outside the group. The collective or
group consciousness can center around entirely different groups, of which some have
a more permanent character — the family, the
class, the clan, the caste, the village, the sect,
the religion, etc. — whereas others are of a
more or less passing character — schoolmates,

a football team, or passengers on a ship. In each case, varying with its permanence, this group-consciousness will strive toward creating homogeneity within the group — a conformity and likemindedness which will lead to and facilitate concerted action. In that sense, we may speak of a group mind and a group action. We may speak of a Catholic mind and Catholic action, of an English mind and English action, but we may also speak of a rural mind or an urban mind, and of action of rural groups or urban groups. All these groups develop their group character. The character of an occupational group, such as peasants, or soldiers, or civil servants, may be as clearly defined and stable as any character of a national group, or more so. Each group creates its own symbols and social conventions, is dominated by social traditions, which find their expression in the public opinion of the group.

Group consciousness is never exclusive. Men find themselves members of different groups at the same time. With the growth of the complexity of civilization, the number of

groups of which men find themselves a part
generally increases. These groups are not
fixed. They have changing limits, and they
are of changing importance. Within these
pluralistic, and sometimes conflicting, kinds
of group-consciousness there is generally one
which is recognized by a man as the supreme
and most important, to which therefore, in
the case of conflict of group loyalties, he
owes supreme loyalty. He identifies himself
with the group and its existence, frequently
not only for the span of his life, but for the
continuity of his existence beyond this span.
This feeling of solidarity between the individual and the group may go, at certain
times, as far as complete submergence of the
individual in the group. The whole education of the members of the group is directed
toward a common mental preparedness for
common attitudes and common actions.

In different periods of history, and in different civilizations, we find different groups
to which this supreme loyalty is given. The
modern period of history, which started with
the French Revolution, is characterized by

the fact that in this period, and in this period alone, the nation demands the supreme loyalty of man; that all men, not only certain individuals or classes, are drawn into this common loyalty; and that all civilizations, which up to this modern period have followed their own, and frequently widely different, ways, are now dominated more and more by this one supreme group-consciousness, nationalism.

It is a fact often commented upon that this growth of nationalism and of national sectionalism took place in the nineteenth and twentieth centuries, just at the time when a growth of international relations, trade, and communications was developing as never before; that local languages were raised to the dignity of literary and cultural languages just at the time when it seemed most desirable to efface all differences of language by the spread of world languages. This view overlooks the fact that it was this very growth of nationalism all over the earth, with its awakening of the masses to participation in political and cultural life, that prepared the way for the closer cultural contacts of all the civilizations of mankind, now for the first time brought into a common denominator — that which at the same time separated and united them.

Nationalism as a group-consciousness is therefore a psychological and a sociological fact, but any psychological or sociological explanation is insufficient. An American psychologist defined a nation as "a group of individuals that feels itself one, is ready within limits to sacrifice the individual for the group advantage, that prospers as a whole, that has groups of emotions experienced as a whole, each of whom rejoices with the advancement and suffers with the losses of the group. . . . Nationality is a mental state or community in behavior." [3] This definition is valid, as far as it goes, not only for the nation but for any other supreme group to which man owes loyalty and with which he identifies himself. It is therefore not sufficient to distinguish the national group from other groups of similar importance and prominence.

Nationalities are the product of the historical development of society. They are not identical with clans, tribes, or folk-groups — groups of men united by actual or supposed common descent or by a common habitat. Ethnographic groups like these have existed throughout history — from earliest times on — yet they do not form nationalities; they are nothing but "ethnographic material," out of which, under certain circumstances, a nationality might arise. Even if a nationality arises, it may disappear again, absorbed in a larger or new nationality. Nationalities are products of the living forces of history, and therefore always fluctuating, never rigid. Nationalities are groups of very recent origin, and therefore of utmost complexity. They defy exact definition. Nationality is an historical and a political concept, and the meaning of the words "nation" and "nationality" has undergone many changes. The words used before the nineteenth century denoted something very different from the modern meanings in the age of nationalism. It is only in recent history that man has started to regard nationality as a center of his political and cultural activity and life. Nationality is therefore nothing absolute; and the greatest mistake, responsible for most of the extremities of today, is to make it an absolute, an objective *a priori* which is a source of all political and cultural life.

Nationality has been raised to an absolute by two fictitious concepts which have been accepted as having real substance. One holds that blood or race is the basis of nationality, and that it exists eternally and carries with it an unchangeable inheritance; the other sees the *Volksgeist* as an ever-welling source of nationality and all its manifestations. These theories offer no real explanation of the rise and the rôle of nationality; they refer us to mythical, prehistorical pseudo-realities. Rather, they must be taken as characteristic elements of thought in the age of nationalism, and are subject themselves to analysis by the historian of nationalism.

3

Nationalities come into existence only when certain objective bonds unite a social group. These bonds are most frequently used for the definition of nationality, but none is essential for the existence of a nationality. A nationality generally possesses several of these attributes; very few possess all of them. Usually the following attributes are enumerated: common descent, language, territory, political entity, customs and traditions, and religion. A short discussion will suffice to show that none of these attributes is essential for the existence or definition of nationality.

Common descent seemed of great importance to primitive man, for whom birth was as great a mystery as death, and therefore surrounded by legends and superstitions. Most modern nationalities, however, are mixtures of different, and sometimes even very distant, races. The great migratory movements of history and the mobility of modern life have led everywhere to an intermingling, so that few if any nationalities can at present claim anything approaching common descent.

The importance of language for the formation and life of a nationality was stressed by Herder and Fichte. But there are many nationalities that have no language of their own — the Swiss, for example, who speak four different languages, or the Latin American nationalities, all of which speak Spanish or Portuguese. The English-speaking nations — Great Britain, the United States, Canada — and the Spanish-speaking nations of Latin America are mostly of common or similar descent; they speak the same language, and until quite recently had the same historical background as well as traditions and customs very much akin to each other; yet they represent different nationalities, with frequently conflicting aspirations. Another example of the comparative irrelevance of objective criteria for the formation and continued existence of separate nationalities is to be found in Norway and Denmark, where the people are most probably of common racial stock and speak almost the same language. Nevertheless, they consider themselves two nationalities, and the Norwegians set up their own language only as the result of their having become a nationality.

Customs and traditions were first stressed in their importance for nationalities by Rousseau. Each nation undoubtedly possesses its customs, traditions, and institutions; but these often vary greatly from locality to locality, and on the other hand tend in our times to become standardized all over the world, or at least over large areas. Customs and manners nowadays often change with great rapidity.

Religion was a dominating force before the rise of nationalism in modern times. This is true of Western as well as Eastern Christianity, of Islam, and of India. The dividing lines were not drawn according to nationalities. Therefore the rise of nationalities and of nationalism was accompanied by transformations in the religious attitude of men, and in many ways the growth of nationalities has been helped or hindered by the influence of religion. Religious differences sometimes divided and weakened nationalities, and even helped to create new nationalities, as in the case of the Catholic Croats and the Orthodox Serbs. On the other hand, national churches have frequently been an important element in helping to arouse nationalism; and when conflicting nationalities were of different religions, religion often played a large part in the defense mechanism of the weaker nationality, as did Catholicism in Ireland and in Prussian Poland.

The most important outward factor in the formation of nationalities is a common territory, or rather, the state. Political frontiers tend to establish nationalities. Many new nationalities, like the Canadian, were formed entirely because they comprised a political and geographic entity. Generally we may say, for reasons which will be considered later, that statehood or nationhood (in the generally accepted sense of common citizenship under one territorial government) is a constitutive element in the life of a nationality. The condition of statehood need not be present when a nationality originates, but in such a case (as with the Czechs in the late eighteenth century) it is always the memory of a past state and the aspiration toward statehood that characterizes nationalities in the age of nationalism.

Although it may be said in conclusion that some of these objective factors are of great importance for the formation of nationalities, the most essential element is a living and active corporate will. Nationality is formed by the decision to form a nationality. Thus the French nationality was born of the enthusiastic manifestation of will in 1789. A French nation, the population of the French kingdom, existed before, as also existed some of the objective conditions necessary for the formation of a nationality. But only the newly aroused consciousness and will made these elements active and effective, fused them into a source of immense centripetal power, and gave them a new importance and meaning. The English and American nationalities were constituted by covenants, by free acts of will, and the French Revolution evolved the plebiscite as a result of which membership in a nationality was determined, not by objective characteristics, but by subjective declaration. The foundation of the Swiss nationality, as dramatized by Friedrich Schiller in his *Wilhelm Tell*, was the legendary oath on the Rütli: "Wir wollen sein ein einig Volk von Brüdern" ("We wish to be one single nation of brothers").

This mythical declaration has been uttered at the birth of every nationality, whether the birth occurred after a long pregnancy in the enthusiasm of a revolutionary period, or whether the awakening of the masses took many years of ceaseless propaganda. Nationalities as "ethnographic material," as "pragmatic" and accidental factors in history, have existed for a very long time; but only through the awakening of national consciousness have they become volitional and "absolute" factors in history. The extensive use of the word "nationality" must not blind us to the fact that the lack of the voluntary element makes what are sometimes called "nationalities" before the rise of modern nationalism something fundamentally different from nationalities at the present time. To base nationality upon "objective" factors like race implies a return to primitive tribalism. In modern times, it has been the power of an idea, not the call of blood, that has constituted and molded nationalities.

Nationalities are created out of ethnographic and political elements when nationalism breathes life into the form built by preceding centuries. Thus nationalism and nationality are closely interrelated. Nationalism is a state of mind, permeating the large majority of a people and claiming to permeate all its members; it recognizes the nation-state as the ideal form of political organization and the nationality as the source of all creative cultural energy and of economic well-being. The supreme loyalty of man is therefore due to his nationality, as his own life is supposedly rooted in and made possible by its welfare. A short discussion of the components of this definition will help to clarify the issues involved.

A state of mind of the large majority of the

people. Even before the age of nationalism, we find individuals who profess sentiments very much akin to nationalism. But these sentiments are confined to individuals; the masses never feel their own life — culturally, politically, or economically — dependent upon the fate of the national group. Periods of oppression or danger from the outside may arouse a feeling of nationalism in the masses, as happened in Greece during the Persian wars and in France during the Hundred Years' War. But these sentiments pass quickly. As a rule, wars before the French Revolution did not arouse a deep national sentiment. In religious and dynastic wars, Germans fought against Germans and Italians against Italians without any realization of the "fratricidal" nature of the act. Soldiers and civilians entered the services of "foreign" rulers and served them, often with a loyalty and faithfulness which proved the absence of any national sentiment.

The nation-state as the ideal form of political organization. That political boundaries should coincide with ethnographic or linguistic frontiers is a demand of recent times. Formerly, the city or the fief or a multi-lingual state held together by dynastic ties was the accepted form of political organization, and frequently was regarded as the "natural" or ideal form. At other periods, the educated classes as well as the masses believed in the ideal of a universal world-state, although on account of the technical and geographic conditions this ideal never approached realization.

The nationality as the source of cultural life. During most of historical time, religion was regarded as the true source of cultural life. Man was thought to become creative by his profound immersion in religious tradition and by his abandonment into the divine fountainhead of all being. At other times, the basis of man's education was steeped in the civilization of a class which spread beyond all national boundaries, like the civilization of knighthood in mediaeval Europe or of the French court in the seventeenth and eighteenth centuries. During and after the Renaissance, man's education was rooted in the soil of classical civilization. Education and learning, the formation of man's mind and character, were not bound by any national limits.

The nationality as a source of economic well-being. This phase of nationalism, as well as the political, was prepared by the period of absolute monarchy, with its mercantilism. But mercantilism never became more than a scheme imposed from above, trying to achieve a national unity which it in reality never approached; continuing in many ways the mediaeval confusion and disruption of economic life; and leaving provinces, cities, and villages as centers of economic life. The purpose of mercantilism was to strengthen the state and its power in international politics. The system following mercantilism, in the period of laissez faire, had as its aim the promotion of individual welfare. Economic nationalism brought about a neo-mercantilism, filling with life, as had been the case with the centralized state, the form erected by the monarchs. It is a much younger development than political or cultural nationalism, and it holds that the well-being of the individual can be achieved and secured only by the economic power of the nation. The close political and cultural identification of the individual with his nationality which took place at the end of the eighteenth and beginning of the nineteenth century extended to the economic field during the latter part of the nineteenth century.

The supreme loyalty due to the nationality. The Austrian monarchy was generally accepted as long as man's supreme loyalty was due to the legitimate king; its existence became precarious with the shift of loyalty from the dynasty to the nationality. Only a very few centuries ago, man's loyalty was due to his church or religion; a heretic put himself beyond the pale of society in the same way that a "traitor" to his nation does today. The fixation of man's supreme loyalty upon his nationality marks the beginning of the age of nationalism.

4

Nationalism is a state of mind. The process of history can be analyzed as a succession of changes in communal psychology, in the attitude of man toward all manifestations of individual and social life. Such factors as language, territory, traditions — such sentiments as attachment to the native soil, the *Heimat*, and to one's kin and kind — assume different positions in the scale of values as communal psychology changes. Nationalism is an idea, an *idée-force*, which fills man's brain and heart with new thoughts and new sentiments and drives him to translate his consciousness into deeds of organized action. A nationality is therefore not only a group held together and animated by a common consciousness; but it is also a group seeking its expression in what it regards as the highest form of organized activity, a sovereign state. As long as nationality is not able to attain this consummation, it satisfies itself with some form of autonomy or pre-state organization, which, however, always tends at a given moment, the moment of "liberation," to develop into a sovereign state. Nationalism demands the nation-state; the creation of the nation-state strengthens nationalism; here, as elsewhere in history, we find a continuous interdependence and interaction.

"Nationality is a state of mind corresponding to a political fact,"[4] or striving to correspond to a political fact. This definition reflects the genesis of nationalism and of modern nationality. Modern nationality was born in the fusion of a certain state of mind with a certain political form. The state of mind, the idea of nationalism, imbued the form with a new content and meaning; the form provided the idea with the implements for the organized expression of its manifestations and aspirations. Both the idea and the form of nationalism were developed before the age of nationalism. The idea goes back to the ancient Hebrews and Greeks, and was revived in Europe at the time of the Renaissance and the Reformation; during the period of the Renaissance the *literati* rediscovered Greco-Roman patriotism; but this new atti-

tude never penetrated to the masses, and its
secularism was soon swept away by the re-
theologization of Europe through the Reformation and Counter-Reformation. But the
Reformation, especially in its Calvinistic
form, revived the nationalism of the Old
Testament. Under the favorable circumstances which had developed in England, a
new national consciousness of England as
the godly people penetrated the whole nation
in the revolution of the seventeenth century.[5]
Meanwhile a new political power — that of
the absolute kings — had developed a new
political form, the modern centralized sovereign state; and this became the political
form into which, during the French Revolution, the idea of nationalism was infused, thus
filling that form with a consciousness in which
all citizens could share and making possible
the political and cultural integration of the
masses in the nation. With the advent of
nationalism, the masses were no longer in the
nation, but of the nation. They identified
themselves with the state, civilization with
national civilization, their life and survival

with the life and survival of the nationality. Nationalism thenceforward dominated the impulses and attitudes of the masses, and at the same time served as the justification for the authority of the state and the legitimation of its use of force, both against its own citizens and against other states.

Sovereignty has a two-fold significance. One aspect deals with the relations of the state to its citizens, the other with the relations between state and state. Similarly, the sentiment of nationalism is double-faced. Intranationally, it leads to a lively sympathy with all fellow members within the nationality; internationally, it finds its expression in indifference to or distrust and hate of fellow men outside the national orbit. In intranational relations, men are guided not only by supposedly permanent common interests, but also by sentiments of sympathy, devotion, and even self-sacrifice, which a crisis tends to intensify. In their international relations, they are guided by the supposed lack of permanent common interests between different states, and by sentiments which vary from the point of complete indifference to the most bitter antipathy, and are subject to swift changes within that range. Nationality, which is nothing but a fragment of humanity, tends to set itself up as the whole.[6] Generally this ultimate conclusion is not drawn, because ideas pre-dating the age of nationalism continue to exercise their influence. These ideas form the essence of Western civilization — of Christianity as well as of enlightened rationalism: the faith in the oneness of humanity and the ultimate value of the individual. Only fascism, the uncompromising enemy of Western civilization, has pushed nationalism to its very limit, to a totalitarian nationalism in which humanity and the individual disappear and nothing remains but the nationality, which has become the one and the whole.

5

Important periods of history are characterized by the circumference within which the sympathy of man extends. These limits are neither fixed nor permanent, and changes in them are accompanied by great crises. In the Middle Ages, the people of the Île de France felt a violent antipathy and contempt for the people of Aquitaine or Burgundy. A short time ago, a similar feeling existed in Egypt between the Mohammedans and the Copts, or native Christians. In ancient times, the Athenians hated and despised the Spartans. Almost unscalable barriers separated members of rival religious sects within a community. In China, until very recently, the family set the limit of sympathy, and very little if any loyalty and devotion were left for the nation or larger social group.

Beginning with the nineteenth century in the Western world, with the twentieth century in the Orient, the circumference was set by the nationality. These changes involved in many cases the establishment of new dividing lines. This grouping of men into new forms of organization, their integration around new symbols, gained a momentum unknown in former days. The rapid growth of population, the spread of education, the increased influence of the masses, the new techniques developed for information and propaganda, gave the new feeling of nationality a permanent intensity which soon made it appear the expression of something "natural," of something which had always existed and would always exist. But there is no assurance that the circumference of sympathy will forever remain drawn as it is today. With the transformation of social and economic life, with the growing interdependence of all nationalities on a shrinking earth, with a new direction to education, the circumference may widen to include supranational areas of common interest and common sympathy.

Such an extension of solidarity, should it come, will arise only as the result of a struggle of unprecedented dimensions. For nationalism represents "vested interests," not only political and economic, but also intellectual and emotional, of an intensity and an extent shown by no previous idea. In the face of the omnipotence of nationality, humanity seems a distant idea, a pale theory or a poetic dream, through which the red blood of life does not pulsate. And so it is. But at one time in history the French or the German nation was also nothing more than a dim idea. Historical forces, amid great struggles and convulsions lasting for a long period, brought these ideas to life. An organization of mankind was a utopia in the eighteenth century; the stage of development of state and economy, of technique and communication, was in no way adequate at that time to the task. It is far different today. At the present time, the sovereignty of nation-states to which we still cling threatens to plunge mankind into repeated catastrophes; nationalism — at its beginning a great and inspiring force, widening and deepening the understanding of man, the feeling of solidarity, the autonomous dignity of the masses — seems unable to cope with the new situation. Once it increased individual liberty and happiness; now it undermines them and subjects them to the exigencies of its continued existence, which is no longer justified. Once it was a great force of life, spurring on the evolution of mankind; now it threatens to become a dead weight upon the march of humanity.

Neither the German nor the French nation

is an entity predestined by nature, any more
than the American nation is. They all, as well
as the national consciousness which animates
them, are formed by historical forces. The
growth of the German national consciousness, the formation of the German national
state, encountered innumerable difficulties
and was again and again in danger of being
wrecked on the cliffs of political vested interests, or the inertia of traditions and of ingrained sectionalism and provincialism. The
pioneers of nationalism were compelled many
times to despair of achieving their goal. But
nationalism was victorious. It was then a progressive principle, a great liberating force,
filling the hearts of men with great hope of a
new freedom and of better and more humane
relations between peoples. This has changed.
"Political nationalism is under present conditions, and in so far as it aims at the creation
of a multitude of uninational states, impossible. It is also undesirable. It conflicts with
the main trends of human affairs, which
are away from isolation towards interdependence. Nationalism is in politics a bitterly

reactionary thing. Its aim is not service and coöperation, but exclusiveness and monopoly. The world needs, not more tariff walls and fortress-barriers, but fewer. The political problem of our day is two-fold. We have, on the one hand, to secure democracy, self-government; on the other, administrative areas which correspond to the social needs of our civilization." [7]

This criticism may be accepted today by a growing number of people. But nationalism is more strongly entrenched at present than it was a short time ago. The nation-state is more deep-rooted in the emotions of the masses than any previous political organization. The growth of nationalism has influenced historiography and the philosophy of history, and each nation has developed its own interpretation of history which not only makes it feel itself different from all other nationalities, but gives to this difference a fundamental, and even metaphysical, meaning. The nationality feels itself chosen for some special mission, and the realization of this mission essential to the march of history, and even to the salvation of mankind. By the identification of nation and state, for which the modern basis was prepared by Rousseau, the cultural and emotional life of the masses has become closely integrated with the political life. Any change of the principles of political organization will therefore encounter the strongest resistance, which will not take into account considerations of the rational and universal good, but will appeal to the vested traditions.

Sociologists have pointed out the intimate relation between national and religious movements. Both have an inspirational, and sometimes revivalist, character. "Both of them are fundamentally cultural movements with incidental political consequences." [8] We should not, however, term the political consequences incidental; rather, they have been conditioned by the stages of historical development. At a given time in history, religion, essentially a spiritual movement, had very fundamental and substantial political implications. Religion dominated politics.[9] At the present time, the same is true of nationalism. When interminable and ferocious religious wars threatened to destroy human happiness and civilization, the movement of Enlightenment, the wave of rationalism which started about 1680 and dominated the eighteenth century, led to the depolitization of religion. In this process, religion did not lose its true dignity; it remained one of the great spiritual forces, comforting and exalting the human soul. It lost the element of coercion which had been so "natural" to it for many centuries; its connection with the state, with political authority, was severed; religion retreated into the intimacy and spontaneity of the individual conscience. The process of the depolitization of religion was slow. Two centuries from "The Bloudy Tenent of Persecution for Cause of Conscience Discussed in a Conference between Truth and Peace," published by Roger Williams in 1644, had to elapse before, at least in Western Europe, its consequences won general acceptance. A similar depolitization of nationality is conceivable. It may lose its connection with political organization, and remain only as an intimate and moving sentiment. But if that day arrives, the age of nationalism, in the sense in which the term is here employed, will be past.

EMPIRE

THE WAY OF MANKIND

My spirit has pass'd in compassion and determination
 around the whole earth,
I have look'd for equals and lovers and found them
 ready for me in all lands,
I think some divine rapport has equallized me with
 them. . . .

Toward you all, in America's name,
I raise high the perpendicular hand, I make the
 signal. . . .
 WALT WHITMAN, "Salut au Monde!"

Chapter Three

EMPIRE

THE WAY OF MANKIND

IMPERIALISM can best be understood historically by a comparison of the various interpretations of Empire, the goal of all imperialism. An identification of nineteenth-century imperialism with economic exploitation outside one's own national or ethnographic borders might be justified, but for centuries the main motivating force behind imperialism has been, rather, an idea — perhaps the most influential single idea for two thousand years, the ordering of human society through unified dominion and common civilization. Today the Reich, though its concept is steeped in the vague darkness of irrational depth, owes its attraction for many minds to the fact that it continues an aspiration which was, during the formative stage of Western civilization, the expression of men's rational hopes. But the Reich, resuming an ancient trend, perverts it into its opposite. For the imperial idea has always rested on Stoic and Christian foundations.

Among the peoples of antiquity the Greeks were not distinguished by military superiority or heroic courage, but by their sense of political liberty and their hatred of authoritarian despotism, their delight in rational thought, and their recognition of universal ethical standards.[1] While the classical Greek thinkers still looked upon the differences between Greeks and barbarians as permanent and fundamental, reserving the possibility of rational thinking and ethical acting to the Greeks alone,[2] Aristotle's pupil, Alexander, disregarding the admonitions of his teacher, set out to unite all men in a new community of civilization. Plutarch has pointed out that Alexander was the first to give effect to the Stoic philosophy of Zeno: that we should consider all men to be of one community and of one order common to all. "For Alexander did not follow Aristotle's advice to have regard for the Greeks as for friends and kindred, but to conduct himself towards other peoples as though they were plants or animals; for to do so would have been to cumber his leadership with numerous battles and banishments and festering seditions. But as he believed that he came as a mediator for the whole world, he brought together in one body all men everywhere, uniting and mixing in one great loving cup, as it were, men's lives, characters, marriages, the very habits of life. He bade them all consider as their fatherland the whole inhabited earth, as akin to them all good men; clothing and food, marriage and manner of life they should regard as common to all, being blended into one by ties of blood and children." [3]

Out of this soil grew the Stoic philosophy and the Roman imperial idea. The Stoic philosophy enriched the Latin language with the new word *humanitas*, an individual norm for man to cultivate the human in him, and a universal norm, the consciousness of the human quality common to all human beings. The whole earth seemed destined

to become one city, with a common civilization which all shared and to which all contributed, and with a common rational law
superseding all the previous tribal differen-
tiations of customs and rights. This static
ecumenical concept was transformed by the
dynamism of the prophetic message of
Christianity; out of their fusion developed
later the rational concepts of liberty and
equality.

In the prevailing state of technology, a
universal empire assuring peace and justice
to all was impossible of achievement; great
distances could not be overcome, and the
adaptation of democracy to large masses and
vast territory by a representative and federal
system was not envisaged. Outside the Empire and within, barbarian masses remained
culturally unintegrated. But in spite of all
its imperfections, the Empire remained for
many centuries the great political inspiration
of mankind, the promise to which men looked
back longingly and which they strove to re-
build to escape self-annihilation by eternal
combat. Even in its full decay, after the sack

of Rome by the Goths, a Gaul, Claudius
Rutilius Namatianus, sang its praise in unforgettable words:

> Fecisti patriam diversis gentibus unam;
> Profuit injustis te dominante capi.
> Dumque offers victis proprii consortia juris,
> Urbem fecisti quod prius orbis erat. . . .[4]

The Roman Empire was destroyed by Germanic tribes who established their rule over
all the known earth. They could not replace
the Empire in its Stoic or Christian form,
because the foundation of civilization, a universal moral law, was unknown to them. To
use the words of a German historian of our
day: "The German way was not the need
for salvation, which was unknown to them.
Nor was it the quest for a moral law; that
they carried within them as will to courageous self-assertion and protection of tribal
honor." [5] The Visigoth Ataulf, Alaric's suc-
cessor, "at first ardently desired to blot out
the Roman name and to make all the Roman
territory in fact as well as in name a Gothic
empire, so that, to use the popular expression,
Gothia should take the place of *Romania*.

Having discovered from long experience that the Goths, because of their unbridled barbarism, were utterly incapable of obeying laws, and yet believing that the state ought not to be deprived of laws without which a state is not a state, he chose to seek for himself at least the glory of restoring and increasing the renown of the Roman name, wishing to be looked upon by posterity as the restorer of the Roman Empire, since he could not be its transformer." [6] Thereafter, all efforts at civilizing the Germans were undertaken by heirs of Roman imperialism. As a renovator of universal civilization Charlemagne subdued the Saxons. When after his death the Empire was divided and the seeds sown for the growth of a parochial instead of a universal loyalty, Florus Lugdunensis lamented in his *Querela de divisione imperii* the end of unity which left *pro regno fragmina regni*,[7] an order fragmentary not only in the political but also in the spiritual sense.

This fragmentary order was rejected by the thought of the Middle Ages, which found

its supreme voice in Dante's faith in the oneness of the *civilitas humani generis*, shortly
before the world center shifted from the
heart of the Empire to its furthest outskirts,
Spain and England. There an imperialism
grew up, directed no longer primarily to the
past hallowed by history, but to the future
and the unknown, fixed with a new spirit of
adventure on lands far beyond the dreams of
any Roman emperor. Even the winds that
blew over these immense spaces carried a
strong scent of the eternal Rome and of the
new Jerusalem. Charles the Fifth was the
last emperor in the traditional sense, as his
grandfather had been the last knight.[8] But
the traditional concept of Empire became
untenable. With the widening *orbis ter-
rarum* the distances seemed to erect insuper-
able barriers; with the revelation of great
civilizations outside Christendom, the old
concept of the *res publica christiana* was no
longer self-evident. A new concept of imperialism emerged, empires knowing themselves definitely as parochial organizations,
as only parts of the whole; and with this

concept came the new phenomenon of conflicting imperialisms and empires, not as
claimants for one and the same office, but
as legitimate competitors within a system of
balance of power. Tommaso Campanella, in
his *De monarchia hispanica*, at the end of the
sixteenth century still regarded Spain as a
basis for an *imperium mundi* in Dante's tradition. Against Machiavelli he pleaded for
the reunion of mankind in a universal spiritual and political unity. He visualized a Spanish monarchy as a great civilizing force, like
Alexander the Great, mixing and assimilating
all races, treating the Indians as brethren
and training some of them in Spain as peasants and artisans. But before long he realized
the utopian character of his hope and of his
confidence that Spain could embody it.

2

The old imperialism was irrevocably dead;
in the seventeenth century England rose as
the foremost representative of the new imperialism. Though far removed from the old
seats of power and civilization, she was

favored in the new age by geographic and economic conditions, by the character of her people, and by the fortuitous blending of the two new forces of the age, the enthusiasm of the Reformation and the enterprise of the new commercialism. Though in the sobriety of the dawning Enlightenment, English imperialism abandoned all claims to world empire, it retained, largely through the Puritan revolution, the Stoic and Christian basis of the old imperialism. English imperialism accepted the new age of contending states. Empire could now be shared with other nations; its foundations, based on universal Christian and rational principles, were not peculiar to England — they were general human principles, destined ultimately, through a process of education, even for the subject races. The thought of Milton and Locke centered in the idea of liberty, individual liberty for Englishmen primarily, but human liberty ultimately.[9]

Of Milton's great battle it has been said rightly that it "was fought for no single generation, for no single land. The destinies of the human race were staked on the same task with the freedom of the English people. Then were first proclaimed those mighty principles which have since worked their way into the depths of the American forests, and which have kindled an unquenchable fire in the hearts of the oppressed, and loosed the knees of the oppressors with an unwonted fear." [10] And Locke started his first *Treatise of Government* with the very sentence which may be regarded as its essence: "Slavery is so vile and miserable an estate of man, and so directly opposite to the generous temper and courage of our nation, that it is hardly to be conceived that an 'Englishman,' much less a 'gentleman,' should plead for it." More than one hundred years later, in the great debate on the abolition of the slave trade, on April 2, 1792, Pitt carried Milton's and Locke's ideas to their logical conclusion: "If we listen to the voice of reason and duty, some of us may live to see a reverse of that picture, from which we now turn our eyes with pain and regret. We may live to behold the natives of Africa engaged in the calm occupations of industry, in the pursuits of a just and legitimate commerce. We may behold the beams of science and philosophy breaking in upon their land. Then we may hope that even Africa shall enjoy at length those blessings which have descended so plentifully upon us in a much earlier period of the world."

These new concepts of liberalism and imperialism did not remain, and were not intended to remain, confined to England; they spread over the earth. Their imperial expansion was based primarily not on glorified state power but on individual initiative; though the political element was not lacking, its motivation was more economic than political. As has been contemptuously said by the theorists of fascist imperialism, the imperialism of the eighteenth and nineteenth centuries was an imperialism of money, not of blood. Money was the rational and universal means of exchange in a world of free and unlimited trade intercourse. Edward Young in his *Imperium Pelagi* has given to this universal harmony of commercial interchange a cosmic expression:

> Kings, merchants are in league and love;
> Earth's odours pay soft airs above,
> That o'er the teeming field prolific range.
> Planets are merchants; take, return,
> Lustre and heat; by traffic burn:
> The whole creation is one vast exchange.

This imperialism felt the restraint not only of a rational business civilization, but also of its Christian and liberal foundations. Often no more than lip service was paid them, and sometimes not even that; but the tradition was strong enough to impose moderation and to rise again and again in ardent protest against all the inhumanities and exploitation involved in modern imperialism. This was true in Great Britain and in the United States,[11] in France and in Germany. Though Canada lay open to the vastly superior forces of her southern neighbor,[12] her unprotected frontier sometimes tempted, yet never invited actual conquest. Though the rich Dutch East Indies were potentially an easy prey for the British fleet, the Netherlanders but rarely felt any apprehension on this point; the Boer war, much protested in Great Britain, was followed by a complete reversal in public feeling and the election of a Liberal government which promptly gave full self-government to the defeated Boers. Even in Germany public indignation forced the repeal of General von Trotha's order of October 2, 1904, to shoot every Herero and to fire indiscriminately on women and children; and in the summer of 1905 von Trotha was superseded by von Lindequist and his more conciliatory policy.[13] The liberal imperialism of the nineteenth century was not only controlled by the recognized plurality of empires and by the restraining force of the acknowledged validity of universal ethical standards, but its inner logic led to its own withering away. The process of decolonization, of increasing concessions to the independence of colonial peoples, had begun well before the outbreak of the Second World War; it augured a possible gradual ascendancy of liberalism over imperialism in that amalgamation which we call liberal imperialism, a

logical contradiction, if we forget the frailty
of human nature and the complexity of all
political life.

3

While in the West a new form of imperialism arose, the medieval idea of world empire
continued in Germany and developed in
Russia, which began to regard itself as the
third Rome, the heir to Byzantium. The
Moscow princes of the sixteenth century assumed the task of continuing the work of
Alexander the Great and of the Roman Empire, "to unite in one organic whole the diverse nations of the East and of the West."
When the Patriarch of Moscow was installed
in 1589, the charter affirmed that "because
the old Rome has collapsed on account of the
heresy of Apollinarius, and the second Rome,
which is Constantinople, is now in possession
of the godless Turks, thy great kingdom, O
pious Tsar, is the third Rome. It surpasses
with its devotion everyone else and all other
Christian kingdoms are now merged in thy
kingdom. Thou art the only Christian sover-

eign in the whole world, the master of all the Christians." [14]

In Germany it was not the princely power but poets and dreamers who kept the imperial dream alive. The German humanists reconstructed a glorious past for their people, not only independent of, but superior to Rome and Christianity. The antiquity of the Germanic tribes and their victorious migrations throughout the world were discovered. The claim to dominion was supported not only historically, but also ethically. The equation of German and good, of alien and evil, led to an exuberance that, in the midst of an ill-defined political reality of historically limitless horizons, fused national state and world empire. While the Renaissance produced new political and social forms in the West, it helped in Germany to preserve the medieval Reich concept. In the words of a contemporary German historian, "the German people, the noblest of the world, chosen by God for the Imperial dignity, the Empire radiant with supernatural splendor, destined for the redemption of mankind from strife and sin, and therefore the necessity of Germanizing the whole world, including the Romance peoples, under the supremacy of the German Emperor — these are the extravagant and exuberant fantasies which on the threshold of modern times cling to the idea of the Reich." [15]

The last great artistic expression, half melancholy and half satirical, of this dream of the future lordship of the world, is found in the fourth chapter of the third book of Grimmelshausen's *Simplicissimus.* There a fool who thinks himself Jupiter speaks of the "German hero" who will come and "conquer the whole world, and make an end of all the godless." He will ask his enemies to submit, and if they refuse, he will execute those whom Hitler calls today the "war-mongers" because they have caused the people not to submit. The foreign princes he will divide into three classes: the wicked ones he will punish; those who are ready to live as commoners under German overlordship he will allow to do so; those, however, who are too proud for that, he will send to Asia where

the German *Kriegsgurgeln* will conquer lands
for them. As for the western Christian kings,
they will not resist, but will receive their
crowns as German fiefs: England, Sweden,
and Denmark because they are of German
race, and Spain, France, and Portugal because the Germans of old conquered them.
Then a perpetual peace will reign between
all nations, and as Grimmelshausen goes on,
"the German people's way of living shall be
more plentiful and comfortable than is now
the life and household of a king." The German hero will not only reorder the world but
also reform all religions into one, by calling
together all the theologians and, if they refuse
to listen to him, forcing them by means of
hunger and the gallows to abandon their
"stiff-necked false doctrines. When Unity is
achieved he will proclaim a great festival and
declare to the whole world his purified religion; and whosoever opposes it, him he will
torment with pitch and sulphur." A fantastic
picture indeed, yet in 1942 the four steps
described by the "fool" — the forceful unification of all German lands, the dynamic ex-

pansion to the East, the easy conquest in the West, and finally the proclamation of a new world-religion — seem less fantastic.

But the eighteenth century dispelled all these dreams: in Russia through Peter the Great, who forced "the third Rome" into the communion of secular Europe; in Germany through the Enlightenment, which brought about an unprecedented flowering of the German spirit in the fields of philosophy, literature and music, and for a time established a German world leadership among the western nations in a common recognition of the universal standards of Stoic and Christian civilization. By the beginning of the twentieth century, German and even Japanese imperialism had adopted all the external forms of liberal imperialism. Both were on the road to a progressive democratization of their constitutional and social life.

But even then observers, penetrating beneath the surface, discerned the peculiar character of German imperialism, shared to an even greater degree by the Japanese variation. While in the western nations individual initiative played a great role in the development of imperialism, in Germany and in Japan the economic structure was tied much more closely to the State and its power politics. The profound analyst of German nationalism, Paul Joachimsen, has pointed out that "German imperialism, the most recent of all, has been of an entirely different kind. It shares with the other imperialisms only its economic origin. . . . The special difficulty of German imperialism consisted in the fact that the German economy . . . , entirely dependent upon the State, had become an instrument of governmental power. Thus economic expansion implied also expansion of state-power in an entirely different sense than, for instance, in England." [16] Similarly that shrewd American observer of the second German Empire, Thorstein Veblen, stated the case of Germany in terms equally applicable to Japan, both representing what he called "dynastic" states: "What makes this German imperial establishment redoubtable, beyond comparison, is the very simple but also very grave combination of circumstances whereby the German people have acquired the use of the modern industrial arts in the highest state of efficiency, at the same time that they have retained unabated the fanatical loyalty of feudal barbarism." [17] But even in 1918 Lenin could accept the peace treaty of Brest-Litovsk, convinced that a victory of Imperial Germany did not imply the annihilation of the defeated adversary, but only territorial cessions and economic concessions, while the sovereignty and freedom of development of the rump state would be left in 1918 to Soviet Russia as in 1871 to Republican France. Lenin regarded all imperialisms as having a common basis and frame of reference, and therefore as ultimately interchangeable, without the future growth of democracy and socialism being thereby impeded.[18] These premises are no longer valid; their acceptance by later socialists under entirely changed circumstances was detrimental to democracy and socialism. For National Socialist imperialism differs fundamentally from that of the nineteenth century.

4

This new imperialism, abandoning the pluralism of the last centuries, returns to the medieval conception of world empire, now at last realizable as a result of the discoveries and technical progress of our age. But it repudiates the ethical and humanitarian foundations of Empire which, since Alexander, have imposed a restraint upon the relations between men and men, even between victors and vanquished — a restraint often not effective, yet never fully and consciously rejected. In this respect the new imperialism, though externally a return to the longing of antiquity and the Middle Ages, yet represents its very perversion. It differs therein from the only similar effort of modern history, namely, Napoleon's attempt to renew the universal empires of Charlemagne and of Alexander. It has been rightly said of Napoleon that "he believed himself capable of conquering the world, as if nothing was unattainable for him, and no limits existed to his career on earth." [19] But he never dreamt of the dominion of one race over others, of the marshaling of the primitive forces of myth and blood against the reign of reason. His idea of world empire stood in direct opposition to everything for which the new world imperialism of today stands. He was no nationalist; as a son of the eighteenth century he wished "to restore and consecrate at last the kingdom of reason, the full development, the whole enjoyment of all human abilities." [20] One of his favorite ideas was "the fusion of nations" on a footing of equality and on the basis of one common civilization. "I wanted to unite them all into one strong national body," he said. "When this was done people could devote themselves to the realization of the ideal, at present only a dream, of a higher civilization. Then there would be no more vicissitudes to fear, for there would be only one set of laws, one kind of opinion, one view, one interest, the interest of mankind." [21]

Napoleon could not achieve his ambition of undoing the division of Charlemagne's Empire or of following Alexander to the

Indus; personal shortcomings, the technical conditions of the period, and his lack of understanding of nationalism were equally responsible.[22] He wished to prevent the coming of the age of nationalism and of contending imperialisms; in reality he hastened its triumphal march across the stage of world history. What he could not foresee was that this very age of nationalism and contending imperialisms would create the basis for a unified world such as had never yet existed; not only by technical developments, but by drawing even the most distant peoples into the orbit of commercial intercourse and of rational civilization.

Nationalism involved the recognition, and often the furtherance, of the national aspirations of other peoples, whose equal rights to cultural self-realization and political self-determination were, at least theoretically, never denied. For Herder, Jefferson, Mazzini or Mill, their own nationalism was incomplete without the nationalism of all other peoples. The national awakening of dormant peoples, of the Slavs and of the Asiatics, was the natural consequence of the imperialism of the nineteenth century. The national movements in India, in Egypt, and in Arabia were due to the influence of western imperialism. It promoted the rise of a native intelligentsia and élite; within the framework of the liberal nineteenth century the extinction even of an oppressed nationality was well-nigh impossible. The program of the Hakatists for the Polish provinces of Prussia failed, not only because it was repudiated by many Germans themselves, but also because the methods employed, though ruthless in theory, were "not ruthless enough to be effective." As a recent historian of the Hakatist movement has remarked, "to dispossess whole populations, a statesman must either annihilate them or have a place to send them; the dissolution of international society is perhaps the prerequisite." [23] The pluralist and commercial imperialism of the nineteenth century presupposed an international society, though it did much to undermine it; the new imperialism demands its dissolution and works for it.

The new imperialism has frequently been misinterpreted as a movement determined by the same economic or nationalistic motives as those of nineteenth-century imperialism. Not only has its universal claim been overlooked, but also its repudiation of the basic concepts of civilization, which makes it an unprecedented phenomenon in history. This very newness explains the pertinacity with which, in spite of all the testimony of its spokesmen, the foundations and aims of the emerging new empire have been misjudged. It does not regard itself as a continuation of "the thousands of years of human domestication" through the restraints imposed by religion and civilization; it inaugurates consciously a new era in which the so-called "iron law of nature" alone will rule. For, as Hitler wrote, "either the world will be ruled according to the ideas of our modern democracy, or the world will be dominated according to the natural law of force; in the latter case the people of brute will will be victorious, and not the nation with self-restraint." Then, to quote Hitler again, "so-called humanity and humanitarianism, which are the expression of a mixture of stupidity, cowardice, and arrogant intellectualism, will melt like snow under the March sun." [24] In this transvaluation of all values, from the consequences of which even its spiritual fathers, Nietzsche and Spengler, would shrink in disgust, the sympathy with human suffering, the recognition of human dignity in every individual, the most powerful restraint upon the beast-of-prey-nature of man, is being systematically eradicated and replaced by an education for pitiless hatred and cold-blooded extermination.[25] The new imperial rule in Poland is praised by the governor-general, Hans Frank, as "the best example of what the new order will look like in countries which are to be spheres of German rule." [26] For Hitler has clearly recognized that "the application of force alone, without the driving power of a great idea behind it, can never bring about the destruction of an idea or arrest its propagation, unless one is ready and able ruthlessly to exterminate the last upholders of that idea even to a man, and also wipe out any traditions which it may tend to leave behind." [27]

Like the old conception of Empire, the new Empire denies the world of nations, not, however, in the sense of fusing all nations under a common law, but in reserving the right to nationalism to the master race alone and assigning all other nations to graded spheres of peculiar laws and circumscribed national self-expression. National development of other peoples is no longer regarded as desirable in itself. "We must promote and welcome nationalism," Rosenberg wrote, "as a manifestation of certain inner values only in those nations the forces of whose future destiny we believe will not come into conflict with the radiations of the German people." With derision he meets the claims of colored peoples for self-determination. "All that does not interest us, or only in so far as a far-sighted German policy expects a strengthening of the German position by using" these aspirations of weaker or inferior races.[28] Similar derision and abuse is heaped by Hitler on the movements for the freedom of oppressed nationalities; Hitler's objections to the British Empire are based upon the argument not that it is brutal or too oppressive, but that it is not brutal or oppressive enough.[29]

Thus the changing concepts of Empire reflect the decisive crisis of the twentieth century. The new imperialism has been so strong because it has realized from the beginning the basic nature of the struggle, the incompatibility of its own principles with those generally acknowledged by civilization. It appealed to one great tradition of western civilization, the longing for a peaceful world order, at the very moment when closeness of intercourse on a shrinking earth rendered a peaceful ordering of otherwise clashing nationalisms imperative. Hitler, who regarded as an unbearable disgrace the peaceful period before the first World War and welcomed the outbreak of war with an unbounded gratitude and enthusiasm,[30] nevertheless had something to say of a peaceful world order: "Who really would desire the victory of pacifism in this world, must work with all his power for the conquest of the world by the Germans. . . . Actually the pacifist humanitarian idea will perhaps be quite good, when once the master man has conquered and subjected the world to a degree that makes him the only master of this earth." [31] But the Empire foreseen by Hitler in these words is a caricature and a complete denial of Western tradition. Perhaps it recalls the *ragna rök*, the fate of the gods, or as the German translation has called it, the *Götterdämmerung*, predicted in the Edda:[32]

> The fetters will burst, and the wolf run free . . .
> Wind time, wolf time, ere the world falls;
> When no man on earth his fellow man shall spare.

The twentieth century may see the end of the era of contending imperialisms and Empires, but if it returns, under new technological conditions and with a wealth of experience in the art of administration, to the ancient concept of Empire, then it will be in the spirit in which Zeno praised Alexander and Claudius Rutilius the Roman Empire, for having afforded to all peoples the equal protection of a common citizenship and of a rational law. This Empire would mean the end of all imperialism,[33] it would be the consummation and the justification of the best tendencies inherent, though not realized, in the liberal imperialisms of the nineteenth century.

CRISIS

THE WAY OF CIVILIZATION

One thought ever at the fore —
That in the Divine Ship, the World,
    breasting Time and Space,
All Peoples of the globe together sail,
    sail the same voyage, are bound to
    the same destination.

WALT WHITMAN, "Old Age Echoes"

Chapter Four

CRISIS

THE WAY OF CIVILIZATION

IN THE YEAR 1936 the crisis, whose roots reach deep into the past and whose outcome will determine the future forms of life, was unveiled for the first time in its all-encompassing character. The approach of the Second World War had been clouded by the mists of the Washington Conference on naval limitation and on the Far East, by the treaty of mutual guarantee between Germany, Belgium, France, Great Britain, and Italy, known as the Locarno Pact of October 16, 1925, and by the general pact for the renunciation of war, the so-called Briand-Kellogg Pact of 1928. This benevolent mist of good intentions and lofty words, hiding the reality of indecision, irresponsibility, and lack of vision, lifted in 1936; the Second

World War had started. From its inception, its actions and implications unrolled on an earth-wide scale. It began in far-off Africa. It did not remain confined there. For what was involved was not a Negro kingdom in Africa, not one of the oldest Christian monarchies on earth, but the principle on which international conduct was to rest.

On July 3, 1935, the Emperor of Ethiopia, in view of Italian threats of war against his country, asked the American government to examine ways and means of securing the observance of the Briand-Kellogg Pact to which all three parties in question had adhered as the cornerstone of a better world. Two days later the American government declared that it "would be loath to believe that either (Italy or Ethiopia, as if these two were equal in that respect!) would resort to other than pacific means as a method of dealing with this controversy or would permit any situation to arise which would be inconsistent with the commitment of the pact." [1] But beyond this righteous hope for Italy's (and Ethiopia's) respect for the pact, America rejected the request for securing its observance. Under this leadership the Briand-Kellogg Pact was wrecked: the war broke out. The League of Nations proposed to put the system of collective security into action; it was done in a half-hearted way. Was it worth while to save the Covenant at considerable inconvenience, even some risk? For a reply to this question it did not matter whether the Ethiopian government was good or the existence of the Abyssinian state desirable. Certainly these questions could have been answered in different and contradictory ways. Some observers might have rightly believed that Ethiopia was a "backward" country lacking many of the moral and technical refinements of "progressive" nations; still, they might be pardoned for doubting whether fascist poison gas, unresisted air bombardments, and mass-executions were the "progressive" way of amending the deplorable situation. On the other hand, there might have been some who thought that there was more hope for improvement in pre-civilized Ethiopia than in the post-civilized corruption and violence of

the fascist aggressors. Yet all these considerations would have been beyond the point;
what mattered was the question of good
faith in the observance of treaties. With the
cornerstone removed, the whole precarious
building of peace threatened to collapse.
But at this juncture of history even more was
at stake than the question of war and peace.
And well it may have been, in keeping with
the character of the crisis, that the continuous chain [2] of the drama began in an act done
"unto one of the least of these my brethren"
and in the condoning of the wrong done to
the Ethiopians.

In vain the Emperor's daughter, Princess
Tsahai, appealed to the foreign journalists in
Addis Ababa on April 27 to mobilize world
opinion: "We are only a small race; but I am
seventeen and its leading daughter, and I
know, as you know, that if mankind lets
armies and gas destroy my country and people, civilization will be destroyed too. We
have common cause, you and I. Why, therefore, do not all do something to drive off this
common danger to humanity, this agony,

this death by bomb, shell, and gas, before it again establishes itself as it is doing here now, soon to spread fatally to your homes and your menfolk too? Italian aggression and gas have set humanity a test. If you fail to help us now, we all shall die." [3] The warning voice of the young Negro woman, a child expressing more wisdom than most of the experienced civilized statesmen of the time, remained as unheeded as that of her father, who two days later told the same simple and fundamental facts to the correspondent of *The Times*: "Do the people of the world not yet realize that by fighting on until the bitter end I am not only performing my sacred duty to my people, but standing guard in the last citadel of collective security? Are they too blind to see that I have my responsibilities to the whole of humanity to face? I must still hold on until my tardy allies appear. And if they never come, then I say prophetically and without bitterness: The West will perish."

The peoples of Europe and of the two Americas did not understand. Nobody was ready to "die for Ethiopia." On May 2, 1936, Haile Selassie left his capital, on May 5 the Italians entered it. On the same day the head of the Italian government proudly proclaimed to the world from the balcony of the Palazzo Venezia: "It is our peace, the Roman peace, which is expressed in this simple, irrevocable, definitive proposition: Abyssinia is Italian — Italian in fact, because occupied by our victorious Italian armies; Italian by right, because with the sword of Rome it is civilization which triumphs over barbarism." What Haile Selassie had regarded as the indication of civilization's mortal crisis, Mussolini claimed as its shining victory. Thus from the onset the Second World War revealed its decisive character as a struggle for much more than some piece of land or some economic goods; it was a struggle for the meaning of civilization. Not only does Signor Mussolini's interpretation of "right" seem far from definitive; even the assertion of the "fact" proved far from "irrevocable." On May 5, 1941, Haile Selassie re-entered Addis Ababa as Emperor, and by the end of the year all Italian troops in the fascist Empire of East Africa had surrendered. But while through the fortunes of war and thanks to the inefficiency of fascism the Italian conquest of Ethiopia achieved in violation of the League of Nations Covenant and of the Briand-Kellogg Pact was undone, the League of Nations had collapsed and the Briand-Kellogg Pact had been revealed as a sham.

On May 11, 1936, the Ethiopian representative in Geneva wrote in a communication to the League of Nations: "The deserted Ethiopian people was smitten with a boundless despair when, at the beginning of March 1936, it realized that it must abandon the hope and the faith that it had placed in the support of the League of Nations." But not only the Ethiopians had reason for despair: in the general inaction more had happened than the abandonment of the Ethiopians. For, as the Archbishop of York pointed out in his presidential address to the York Diocesan Conference on June 25, what had been at stake was not the saving of Ethiopia or anyone else, it was the maintenance of international order.[4] Collective security had failed, not because it was wrong or difficult to carry out, but because the will to try it seriously was lacking. Chancellor Hitler, with his unique genius of detecting and using all the weaknesses and deficiencies in the souls and systems of his adversaries, learned the lesson immediately. On March 7, 1936, he tore up the Locarno Pact. This Pact had not been a "dictate," it had been a freely negotiated treaty which included most valuable and far-reaching concessions to Germany. In his speech before the German Reichstag on May 21, 1935, Chancellor Hitler had called the Locarno Pact "the most definite and most really valuable treaty of mutual assurance in Europe." He had promised on behalf of his German government that "they will scrupulously maintain every treaty voluntarily signed, even though it was completed before their accession to power and office. In particular they will uphold and fulfill all obligations arising out of the Locarno Treaty, so long as the other partners are on their side ready to stand by that pact.

In respecting the demilitarized zone the German government considers its action as a contribution to the appeasement of Europe." The next day *The Times* of London had welcomed the speech editorially and warned sharply against any distrust in Chancellor Hitler's intentions. The editor rejoiced at the thought that the German Führer "declared most solemnly that the German Government would respect unconditionally all the obligations affecting the relations between the German and other governments that had already been assumed, even if they had been assumed before the advent of the National Socialist regime. In this connection Herr Hitler specifically mentions the Locarno Pact. . . . It is to be hoped that the speech will be taken everywhere as a sincere and well-considered utterance, meaning precisely what it says. There are no greater enemies to the peace of Europe than those who would spread an atmosphere of suspicion about an important and long-awaited pronouncement of this kind."

On March 7 the Rhineland was remilitarized by Germany. Probably no single event was of as fateful consequence for the triumph of National Socialist principles on the international stage than this tearing up of the Locarno Pact. The outlook for the future was not improved by Chancellor Hitler's new solemn promise, delivered the same day: "We have no territorial demands to make in Europe. We know above all that the tension resulting from wrong territorial provisions cannot be solved in Europe by wars." At that moment Germany, not yet prepared for war, could have been stopped without any great risk involved. Chancellor Hitler staked his whole future, as well as the future of mankind and of international order, on his judgment of the wisdom and courage of the French, British, and Americans. His judgment did not fail him. His daring, based upon his unbounded contempt for other, and especially for democratic, men, brought him the greatest and most far-reaching success of his whole career. The last shred of security which the victory of 1918 had promised to France, a country devastated and bled white in the war as no other great power, was gone. An effective collaboration between France and her allies to the east and southeast of Germany was made impossible. Central and southeastern Europe was definitely abandoned to Chancellor Hitler's aspirations, whenever he would think the moment had come. Many influential circles in Great Britain were deeply satisfied; some liberals in America rejoiced. They regarded this peaceful settlement as highly preferable to a preventive war, they welcomed what they called a step to remove the "injustices and hatreds of Versailles," and a check upon France's "unjustified and insatiable" desire for security, born out of deep-seated distrust and resentment. Many wondered whether Chancellor Hitler's warnings of the dangers of Bolshevik expansion in Europe were not justified and feared lest resistance drive the Germans into the arms of communism. Hitler appeared to save Germany, and perhaps the world, from this danger. In any case he claimed it. In view of all these circumstances it seemed best to approach the delicate situation "realistically," to distrust all references to ethics, ideologies, and similar far-fetched and disputable concepts and to reduce the situation to the "underlying" familiar notions of economic and territorial aspirations about which one should negotiate; thus peace would be preserved. The notion that the "idealistic" approach through collective security and the observation of treaties was the only foundation on which the reality of peace could be built was scorned by people who liked to call themselves realists.[5]

Simultaneously with the "liquidation" of the League of Nations Covenant, of the Briand-Kellogg Pact, and of the Locarno Pact, the final attempt was prepared to destroy the foundations for peace in the Pacific, laid down in Washington in 1922 and badly shattered in 1931. On February 26, 1936, a number of leading Japanese statesmen became the victims of an uprising by patriotic murderers among the young army officers. Admiral Viscount Makoto Saito, Lord Keeper of the Privy Seal, was stabbed to death and his wife gravely wounded;

the able finance minister Korekiyo Taka-
hashi, and the Inspector-General of Military Education, General Jotaro Watanabe,
were killed; the Grand Chamberlain Admiral
Kantaro Suzuki was wounded; while other
designated victims like Prince Kimmochi
Saionji, the venerable last Genro, Count
Nobuaki Makino, a former Lord Keeper of
the Privy Seal, and the Premier Admiral
Keisuke Okada escaped by ruse and good
luck the fate which the conspirators had prepared for them. After three days of strange
fighting the revolt of the young officers collapsed, but the spirit which animated it, the
struggle against "dangerous thought" (which
ostentatiously meant communism but in reality meant Western liberalism and humanism) triumphed. Though the junior officers
involved in the assassinations were put before a court martial, there was no general or
public condemnation of the murders. It appeared as if the murdered men, not their
assassins had been responsible. "The massa-
cre was immensely popular in the army. The
army acted as though the revolt was the work

of the whole body and had succeeded. In its
new orders the army said that it could not
tolerate liberalism, that internationalism and
individualism must be banished, and nationalism and 'the Japanese principle' promoted." [6] In February 1936 the army definitely took control of Japan, burning with a
faith which seems fantastic to the Western
mind but bears close resemblance to the
tribal mysticism of German nationalism.[7]
The foundations for the China "incident" of
July 7, 1937, were laid.

Thus by 1936 a new "revolutionary" patriotic ardor, feeding upon intolerance and
disregard of human life and divine law, re-
jecting all the restraints which so far had kept
political life within bounds, emerged triumphantly in Italy, Germany, and Japan. Before this new fervor could bear full fruit on
the world stage, the three movements of national and international lawlessness joined
hands. The remilitarization of the Rhineland
convinced Signor Mussolini that the future
belonged to Germany and that the democratic nations would not resist. He was as

aware of the strategic importance of Spain as of the psychological effects of a defeat of liberal forces in a country recently liberated from the grip of a moribund traditionalism — the more so because these liberal forces had achieved an unexpected victory in France in the elections of May 1936 and by their triumph indicated a rejection of the claims of fascist ascendancy. Thus he was eager to co-operate with Chancellor Hitler in supporting military and nationalist rebellion in Spain against the coalition of liberals and socialists who then formed the legal government of the country as they did in neighboring France. When it became apparent that the popular enthusiasm of the Spaniards would defeat the rebellion, Germany and Italy jointly decided to support the rebels until final victory. Rarely were international relations degraded to a more farcical level. The intervention was carried on partly under the pretext that it did not exist at all and partly under the pretence that it was directed against communism. While influential groups in France, Great Britain, and the United

States applauded this commendable crusade against Bolshevik perils, its real goal was to gain control of a strategical and ideological position which would facilitate the disintegration of France, weaken the British position in the western Mediterranean, and endanger the security of the United States in the southern Atlantic and in Latin America. While thus Germany and Italy joined hands in the West for the control of the Mediterranean and the Atlantic, Germany and Japan united in the East for the control of the Pacific. The same pretext did good service there: it found expression in the so-called Anti-Comintern Pact of November 25, 1936. Yet as its result Japan did not attack the Soviet Union; instead, in her expansion, she moved steadily towards the south, toward control of the South Seas and of the rich American, British, and Dutch lands in the western Pacific and the Indian Ocean.

While these preparations for successful conduct of a second, earth-encompassing, World War reached their peak, the United States, having contributed more than its share to the economic disorganization of the world by high tariffs, by insistence on the repayment of war debts, and by its reckless boom-and-crash psychology, debated the perfection of its neutrality legislation. It thus formally informed the German Chancellor and the Japanese army that they would be allowed to go on conquering strategic positions for their final onslaught on the "citadel of liberty." It denied the victims of aggression, who were as unprepared in a military way as the United States, any hope of help, and abandoned them resolutely and righteously to their fate. This legislation, or rather the attitude of mind that it expressed, intensified the belief of the American people that its will to peace and its geographic position guaranteed its security, that it could be involved in war only by "intervention," and that nobody would wish or be able to attack it. The paralysis of mind and will, the cherished illusionism in the interpretation of history, the false sense of security in the United States faithfully resembled the same state of mind in Great Britain, France, and the smaller countries of both hemispheres, thus proving again the essential unity of public reactions all over the earth in the present crisis. This uniformity of response, an essential corollary of the indivisibility of war and peace in our time, showed itself also in each nation's understanding and criticizing the inadequate response of other nations to the challenge of the crisis but rarely recognizing the implications of its own refusal to take the risk of coöperation. The public mind was most productive everywhere in satisfying itself with many good reasons for its independent actions and its "love of peace." This attitude naturally led to mutual distrust and recriminations; it thus helped to divert attention from the common danger and rendered timely and collective action more difficult. It was this state of the public mind everywhere, more than the actions of individual statesmen or nations, which produced the disintegration of collective security.

This disintegration was further accentuated in the fateful year of 1936 by King Leopold III of Belgium, who on October 14,

1936, insisted on the need of a "purely Belgian" foreign policy and dissolved the alliance with France, in spite of the fact that the French General Staff had made all their calculations for the security of France on the assumption that the territory of Belgium and of France would be considered as a single strategic unit. Belgium's return to neutrality paved the way for Chancellor Hitler's generous offer — in his speech to the Reichstag on January 30, 1937 — of a German guarantee of Holland's and Belgium's inviolability "as untouchable and neutral regions for all time." While the Netherlands rejected the German offer, Belgium built her own security (and incidentally that of France and Great Britain) upon Germany's solemn declaration of October 13, 1937, that "in no circumstances will the German government impair the inviolability and integrity of Belgium, and that they will at all times respect Belgian territory, except, of course, in the event of Belgium's taking part in a military action directed against Germany." While this was happening in the West, the system of collective security which had afforded some though precarious safety against aggression in Eastern Europe, crumbled there too. Poland had deserted it already, and under Colonel Josef Beck was hopefully following a foreign policy of coöperation and friendship with National Socialist Germany and Fascist Italy. In Rumania, which had been a staunch supporter of the League of Nations and a friend of France and of Czechoslovakia, the resignation of Nicholas Titulescu as Foreign Minister on August 29, 1936, meant the end of an era. Its background was formed by the exploits of the Legion of Archangel Michael, highly patriotic murderers, who showed in their theories and actions, in spite of wide differences of race and creed, astonishing affinities with their Japanese fellow enthusiasts for nationalism and religion. Rumania now began to follow the policy of neutrality and realistic *rapprochement* with the fascist powers which Colonel Beck seemed to lead so successfully in Poland and Prime Minister Milan Stojadinović, who had been appointed on June 20, 1935, was making more and more to prevail in Yugoslavia. Thus, all over the earth, governments and peoples abandoned — following the lead of the fascist powers — the "chimera of collective security" for the "realism" of a purely national or regional policy.

2

In 1936 the Second World War began with two correlated events: the collapse of collective security, the only force that could have prevented it, and the emergence of a system of collective aggression, successfully inaugurated in the same year by the coöperation of Germany, Italy, and Japan. Once again, on September 30, 1937, Signor Mussolini, having just returned from Berlin, was speaking from his balcony in the Palazzo Venezia; he promised "close solidarity between the two revolutions, the renaissance of Europe, and peace among the peoples worthy of this name." He did not specify which peoples were "worthy of this name." He could not do it, because it depended upon changing circumstances. Only peoples were

worthy of this name who understood readily
the worthy aims of Germany, Italy, and
Japan; no "people worthy of this name"
would ever wish to resist their benevolent intentions for the salvation of civilization and
of mankind. Peoples who were not "worthy
of this name" were clearly tools of communism — except for the period from August 23, 1939, to June 22, 1941 — and had
therefore to be fought and castigated for the
sake of civilization; or they were tools of
Judaism — as Mussolini learned in 1938 and
the Japanese in 1941, while Chancellor Hitler, much more prescient, had known it from
the beginning. The Anti-Comintern Pact
was signed by Italy on November 6, 1937,
with the status of an original signator. Thus
these three powers took upon themselves on
behalf of civilization and humanity the burden of a fight against communism and later
against Judaism. Needless to say, people
who resisted identified themselves with communism and Judaism and thus became enemies of mankind and civilization.

In 1936 an understanding of the situation

on the part of the governments and the peoples of the other nations would not only have
saved peace, but would have put an end to
the fascist world revolution. For at no moment was the hold of Hitler, Mussolini, and
the Japanese army over the destinies of their
own people potentially as tenuous as in 1936.
Mussolini would have fallen with the successful resistance of a not-abandoned Ethiopia,
whereas his victory over the League of Nations and Great Britain immensely strengthened his prestige with the Italians. Hitler
staked his whole future on the militarization
of the Rhineland; had Great Britain and
France lived up to their own obligations, had
the Germans been forced to withdraw under
French and British pressure, as the army was
then prepared to do rather than risk a war,
the immense chain of successes which began
in March 1936 and tied Germany more and
more closely to her invincible leader would
have been broken at the beginning. The
patriotic mass murders of the Japanese army
had created such a tension in Japan, even
alienating the navy, that a strong show of

active sympathy for the Chinese might have restored some of the saner elements in Japan, friends of the murdered victims, to influence. And in the secondary countries, such as Spain and Rumania, the flimsy structure which the native "fighters for civilization and humanity" tried to erect would have collapsed completely and easily without outside assistance. But the liberal and democratic forces, still existing in these countries, were abandoned by France, Great Britain, and the United States to their common enemies. Too many people were interested in the maintenance of the "order" seemingly assured by fascism, or persisted in misunderstanding, sometimes in a sentimental way, the historical forces at work in Germany and Japan.

Thus for almost five years the Second World War was fought with growing success by Germany, Japan, and Italy. Their main adversaries, Great Britain and the United States — adversaries not because they wished to be, but because the political and ideological goal of the three powers could not be achieved without the annihilation of the two

English-speaking democracies — pursued a policy of "peace," wishing at almost any price to avoid armed conflict, and continued to supply their enemies with weapons and resources. No power has ever done more for the preservation of peace and for trying to arrive at a friendly understanding with Germany, Italy, and Japan than Great Britain did until the very moment when no choice was left her but to accept the challenge. The new British ambassador to Berlin, Sir Nevile Henderson, voiced the sentiments of many people in Great Britain, the United States, and other states since attacked openly by Germany, when he deprecated in a speech in Berlin on June 1, 1937, a widespread, but "entirely erroneous conception of what the National Socialist regime really stands for." If the critics of the Third Reich had a truer vision, he said, they would lay less stress on Nazi dictatorship "and much more emphasis on the great experiment which is being tried out in this country." In Sir Nevile's opinion these critics could not see the wood for the trees, while in reality German culture, Ger-

man philosophy, and German ideas were
among the noblest in the world, and German
thoroughness and industry have always been
objects of British admiration.[8] Men like Sir
Nevile Henderson were sincerely devoted to
the cause of an understanding between Great
Britain and Germany, they had similar sym-
pathies for Italy and Japan, they distrusted
or hated the Soviet Union and they were
rather doubtful about the Popular Front in
France and the New Deal in the United
States. They failed in their efforts to arrive
at an understanding with Germany, Italy,
and Japan, because without knowing it they
attempted the impossible. They did not see
that there was no alternative outside determined resistance or full submission; they
completely misunderstood the nature of the
forces with which they had to cope. Even today, when the survival of their own nations
is openly at stake, many of them, though disillusioned in the failure of their efforts to
arrive at an understanding which they called
peace, still do not comprehend the fundamentals of the forces by which they are faced,

or the strength of their antecedents in German and Japanese history and thought. The genuine force of the revolution which National Socialism in all its allied and tributary forms prides itself on being entirely escaped their anti-metaphysical, nineteenth-century minds. Therefore, some blamed the failure of their efforts on evil personalities like Hitler, attributing to them alone what is a fundamental attitude shared by very many millions — not only in Germany — who see in Hitler the most successful representative of a new way of life and a new political philosophy. To others, Germany and Japan seemed to represent strength and thus to guarantee order, a bulwark against chaos, a promise of social stability, while the revolutionary anarchy in Russia and in China and the many new small states with their confusing and conflicting claims seemed to create ever new complexities in a society which had fast grown too complex for the tranquility of mind and the economics of prosperity. From this point it was only one step to the conclusion that, after all, the aggressors might really

do well for civilization and for humanity —
not immediately, because their methods were
somewhat reprehensible, yet ultimately, if
one could only accept what was called the
long-range view; and that, after all, the
victims were the guilty ones because their
disorder or backwardness had invited the
aggression, or because, like all human organizations, they had not been free from guilt
in the past.

This attitude was in no way confined to
men of the "Right" — yet it was a rather
strange spectacle to find the stalwart defenders of Empire and national interests so eager
for "peace" that they lost all understanding
of the strategic implications of power politics
and prestige. Men of the "Left" shared the
fundamental misunderstandings. They often
believed, like Sir Nevile Henderson, that the
Treaty of Versailles had wronged the Germans, that National Socialism was a product
of the Treaty of Versailles, and that some
restitution was due to the Germans. They
were fascinated by German culture and philosophy, or by Japanese esthetic forms, with-

out any deeper knowledge of the tendencies
of German and Japanese history and thought.
They were "convinced" that wars do not set-
tle anything and that all other peoples share
this unhistorical interpretation of history. Although, in common with most men of the
"Right," they deprecated the crude anti-
Semitism and brutality of National Socialism,
they thought National Socialism had good
aspects too. They could not understand that
there are no good or bad aspects to fascism,
that it forms a whole, shaping the minds of
men under its influence into an attitude
fundamentally opposed to all principles of
liberalism and of international coöperation,
and therefore necessarily aggressive against
the democracies. They saw in fascism only
an aberration, caused by the Treaty of Versailles or by economic dislocation, from the
accepted liberal course of modern civilization, and they harbored a deep suspicion
against any sharp division of mankind into
two camps, against any "black and white,"
"devil and angel" dichotomy. Above all,
whether they represented big business or the

proletariat, they were deeply convinced that
the chief motivations of all political and historic life are economic. Nothing has done so
much to confuse the well-meaning opponents
of National Socialism as the economic interpretation of social life and of human aspirations. The fascist youth and the Japanese
soldiers are not animated by "common sense"
notions of peaceful progress and economic
welfare; they live in a world of different and
opposite values, in which all words have
gained a different meaning. National Socialism and Japanese militarism are not of economic origin or due to political circumstances, though the situation helped their
ascendancy to power; they belong to the history of ideas. "In German history ideas can
not be explained in terms of situations. It is
the other way about — the German situation
has to be explained in terms of ideas. National Socialism has not arisen out of the
German situation — the German situation,
and therefore, the German war, have arisen
out of National Socialism," wrote an English
political thinker in a somewhat overemphatic

statement.[9] Yet his statement contains a most important element of truth, which escaped completely the understanding of Right and Left alike.

This obliteration of the cleavage between Left and Right is a sign of the crisis. The masses on the Left were on the whole as blind or as unmoved as the classes on the Right. There were many individual exceptions everywhere. For the crisis is a time of test and trial for the individual. Irrespective of his class or caste, of his party allegiance or profession of faith, man is faced in this crisis with an entirely new and unforeseen situation which demands from him decisions far beyond all sociological, racial, or religious determination. The unawareness of the depth and nature of this crisis, or the refusal to believe in it, caused that intellectual and moral confusion in the democracies which gave the National Socialist propagandists the opportunity to proclaim to the whole world that democracy was obsolete and effete and that fascism was the wave of the future, the only form of organization which corresponded to the need of the modern age of industrial masses.

3

The Second World War is a continuation of the First World War, not as a result of the Treaty of Versailles, but as an effect of the same forces which brought about the First World War. Of course, if Germany had won the First World War and achieved her goal then, there might have been no Second World War. The First World War served Germany and Japan, though they fought in opposite camps (but not one against the other), to the same purpose — an effort to establish positions so overwhelmingly strong that they could not be challenged by any combination of powers and that their hegemony would have to be accepted. Germany tried to do it by creating under the slogan of "Middle Europe" a continental bloc under her domination from the Channel Coast to the Persian Gulf and the Caspian Sea; Japan, by uniting under the Pan-Asiatic war-cry the teeming millions and the vast resources of

Asia and the South Seas. The outcome of the First World War defeated these aspirations. The Treaty of Versailles reversed the development apparently sanctioned in the Treaty of Brest-Litovsk, and the treaties of Washington reduced and confined Japanese expansion. For both these decisions the power of the United States bore the chief responsibility. No wonder that Germany and Japan regarded the United States as the decisive enemy. For both refused to accept the defeat; they saw it only as a temporary setback, and were determined to wait for an opportunity to reassert their aspirations under more auspicious conditions and to be fully prepared for making full use of the new chance to gain their goal.

All this was clearly foreseen by Thorstein Veblen, that most original American social thinker of Norwegian descent, who combined the mid-western populist attitude with a rare acumen and breadth of international vision when he wrote in January 1917 *An Inquiry into the Nature of Peace and Terms of Its Perpetuation*, which like all of his work is indebted to Immanuel Kant. There he pointed out that "chief among the relevant circumstances in the current situation are the imperial designs of Germany and Japan. These two national establishments are very much alike. So much so that for the present purpose a single line of analysis will passably cover both cases. Except as a possible corrective of internal disorders and discontent, neither of the two States 'desires' war; but both are bent on dominion, and as the dominion aimed at is not to be had except by fighting for it, both in effect are incorrigibly bent on warlike enterprise. And in neither case will considerations of equity, humanity, decency, veracity, or the common good be allowed to trouble the quest of dominion. Imperial dominion, in the ambitions of both, is beyond price; so that no cost is too high so long as ultimate success attends the imperial enterprise." He faced clearly the question of how a peace compact could be established with these two powers, which, on account of their feudal character, he called "dynastic" states. "Evidently, in the presence of these two imperial Powers any peace compact will be in a precarious case; equally so whether either or both of them are parties to such compact or not. No engagement binds the dynastic statesman in case it turns out not to further the dynastic enterprise. The question then recurs: how may peace be maintained within the horizon of German or Japanese ambitions? There are two obvious alternatives, neither of which promises an easy way out of the quandary in which the world's peace is placed by their presence: Submission to their dominion, or Elimination of these two Powers."

Veblen envisaged the danger of a negotiated peace which would embrace Germany and Japan intact. Such an arrangement, even if accompanied by a compact of perpetual peace, "will necessarily be equivalent to arranging a period of recuperation for a new onset of dynastic enterprise. For, in the nature of the case, no compact binds the dynastic statesman, and no consideration other than the pursuit of imperial dominion commands his attention." With a rare per-

spicacity Veblen added: "Consummation of
Imperial mastery being the highest and ubiq-
uitously ulterior end of all endeavor, its
pursuit not only relieves its votaries from the
observance of any minor obligations that run
counter to its needs, but it also imposes a
moral obligation to make the most of any
opportunity for profitable deceit and chican-
ery that may offer. In short, the dynastic
statesman is under the governance of a higher
morality, binding him to the service of his
nation's ambition to which it is his dutiful
privilege loyally to devote all his powers of
force and fraud. Democratically-minded
persons may have some difficulty in appre-
ciating the moral austerity of this spirit of
devotion, and in seeing how its paramount
exigence will set aside all meticulous scruples
of personal rectitude and veracity, as being
a shabby withholding of service due. This
attitude of loyalty may perhaps be made in-
telligible by calling to mind the analogous
self-surrender of the religious devotee." [10]

Veblen knew, of course, that neither Germans nor Japanese had any "racial" predis-

position for such behavior. It had been made possible by a groundwork of deep popular sentiment and of corresponding social and political institutions, both of which are the result of a historical growth. They "have been learned, acquired, and are in no cogent sense original with the German people. But both alike and conjointly have come out of a very protracted, exacting and consistent discipline of mastery and subjection." This system of coercive law and order has, as compared "with the degree of mitigation which the like order of things presently underwent elsewhere in western Europe, throughout the historical period preserved a remarkable degree of that character of arrogance and servility which it owes to its barbarian and predatory beginnings." [11] Veblen's reflections were a continuation of the "comparison and correlation between the German case on the one hand, and the English-speaking peoples, on the other hand, considered as two distinct and somewhat divergent lines of the cultural development in modern times" which he had analyzed in his *Imperial Germany and the*

Industrial Revolution.[12] In Germany and in Japan he found the formidable phenomenon of a medieval aggressive ruling class wielding the whole material force of a fully conscious national machine industry.

With an unusual perspicacity, Veblen viewed the situation of America and of the world in 1917 in a way which was just as valid in 1940. "Technological knowledge," he wrote, "has thrown the advantage in military affairs definitely to the offensive, particularly to the offensive that is prepared beforehand with the suitable appliances and with men ready matured in that rigorous and protracted training by which alone they can become competent to make warlike use of these appliances." As a result of the same technological progress, "any well-designed offensive can effectually reach any given community, in spite of distance or other natural obstacles."[13] Veblen thus saw clearly in 1917 that in the present age isolationism is of no avail and that the defensive mentality invites disaster. Already some years before him Mahan had recognized the military superiority of, to use Veblen's terminology, the dynastic and offensive states as against the commercial and defensive states, especially in view of the fact that the imperial powers were ready to coöperate while the defensive powers were weakened by their isolationism. He stressed "the growing power of the German Empire, in which the efficiency of the State as an organic body is so greatly superior to that of Great Britain, and may prove to be to that of the United States. The two English-speaking countries have wealth vastly superior, each separately, to that of Germany; much more if acting together. But in neither is the efficiency of the Government for handling the resources comparable to that of Germany; and there is no apparent chance or recognized inducements for them to work together, as Germany and Austria now work in Europe. The consequence is that Germany may deal with each in succession much more effectively than either is now willing to consider." [14]

Veblen was in no doubt in January 1917 about the necessity for America's help in de-

feating Germany. He recognized clearly that
a German victory in 1917 would have marked
down the United States "for reduction to a
vassal state by the dynastic Empire now engaged with its European adversaries." That
did not mean, of course, that the German
archives contained any definite documents
about this future course; yet the subjugation
of the American republic would have been a
necessary sequence of a German victory, the
actual realization of which would depend "on
the conjuncture of circumstances, chief of
which would have to be the exigencies of imperial dominion shaping the policy of the
Empire's natural and necessary ally in the
Far East." [15] In view of this danger of a concerted German-Japanese aggression against
America, Veblen pointed out that the United
States was not fit to take care of its own case
single-handed, not so much for lack of man-
power or resources, but out of a fundamental
disinclination to devote manpower and resources for a long time completely and exclusively to this purpose; for "a democracy
is not to be persuaded to stand under arms

interminably in mere readiness for a con-
tingency, however distasteful the contin-
gency may be." [16] Thus America was obliged
in her own interest to defeat Germany in
1917 and to unite with other nations to maintain peace, because otherwise, with the new
preponderance of offensive weapons and the
end of isolation, she would sooner or later be
in danger of being caught insufficiently prepared by Germany and Japan and of being
involved in a life-and-death-struggle against
the much superior military skill and preparedness of the two great aggressive powers.
For America is in a more dangerous situation
than any other great democracy. "America is
placed in an extra-hazardous position, between the two seas beyond which to either
side lie the two Imperial Powers whose place
in the modern economy of nations it is to
disturb the peace in an insatiable quest of
dominion. This position is no longer defen-
sible in isolation, under the later state of the
industrial arts, and the policy of isolation
that has guided the national policy hitherto
is therefore falling out of date. It will be

said, of course, that America is competent
to take care of itself and its Monroe Doctrine
in the future as in the past. But that view,
spoken for cogently by thoughtful men and
by politicians looking for party advantage,
overlooks the fact that the modern technology has definitively thrown the advantage to
the offensive, and that intervening seas can
no longer be counted on as a decisive obstacle. On this latter head, what was reasonably
true fifteen years ago is doubtful today, and
it is in all reasonable expectation invalid for
the situation fifteen years hence. The other
peoples that are of a neutral temper may
need the help of America sorely enough in
their endeavours to keep the peace, but
America's need of coöperation is sorer still,
for the Republic is coming into a more precarious place than any of the others."

The United States entered the First World
War, not so much to save others as in a far-
sighted attempt to save herself. At the beginning of 1917 German victory in Europe
seemed almost assured: the Russian armies
were disintegrating, in France defeatism was

growing, Great Britain was threatened by the unrestricted submarine warfare. Germany was justified in expecting that the military hegemony in Europe and the control of the Atlantic Ocean would fall to her as the fruit of victory. This would have meant for the United States a state of perpetual armed vigilance, as strong in the mobilization of manpower and industrial resources for war as the great military establishment of victorious Germany would demand, involving in the long run the loss of what has been termed the American way of life. America would have become the neighbor of Germany on the one hand and the neighbor of Japan on the other hand, a Japan of the same mind and coöperating with Germany. The United States entered the First World War to make the world safe for democracy — not to impose democracy upon others, but to make the world a place in which American democracy would be safe. It was regrettable that the American people did not understand the real reasons for its participation in the World War. Enlightened self-interest is a better guide to national actions than a feeling of missionary charity; the latter easily leads to a holier-than-thou attitude and a wrong perspective in regard to the motivating forces in history; it quickly changes from the lofty idealism of disinterested benefactors of mankind to a disillusioned cynicism which explains history by blaming secret activities of munition makers and bankers. The United States helped to defeat Germany, and by her help saved Great Britain and France and liberated Belgium and Serbia, but she also saved herself. In the crisis America could not save herself without saving others. Her fate was indissolubly linked with that of all non-aggressive nations. Had the people of the United States understood it then, they would have helped to form what Veblen called the "neutral league" in which "national interests and pretensions would have to give way to a collective control [of military force] sufficient to ensure prompt and concerted action." [17] Veblen regarded the participation of the United States and of the United Kingdom as indispensable to the success of the project. Both peoples, the American and the British, balked at the understanding of the situation. As Veblen had foreseen in 1917, the two dynastic Empires could now wait for an opportunity for recuperation and "a wiser endeavor to achieve that dominion" which they had been unable to achieve in the second decade of the twentieth century. The fifth decade of the century found the United States fighting for its very existence against Germany and Japan, Belgium and Serbia again extinguished as independent nations, France a victim of that defeatism which in 1917 raised its ugly head, and Great Britain in a predicament infinitely more fraught with danger than even that of 1917.

And thus in January 1942 America was left to ponder the truth of the words which Veblen wrote in January 1917: "It appears already to be realised in the most responsible quarter that America needs the succor of the other pacific nations, with a need that is not to be put away or put off; as it is also coming to be realised that the Imperial Powers are disturbers of the peace, by force of their Imperial character. Of course, the politicians who seek their own advantage in the nation's embarrassment are commonly unable to see the matter in that light. But it is also apparent that the popular sentiment is affected with the same apprehension, more and more as time passes and the aims and methods of the Imperial Powers become more patent. Hitherto the spokesmen of a pacific federation of nations have spoken of America's share in the project as being that of an interested outsider, a humane solicitude for the well-being of civilised mankind at large. Now, there is not a little verisimilitude in this conception of America as a tower of strength in the projected federation of neutral nations, however pharisaical an appearance it may all have in the self-complacent utterances of patriotic Americans. The American republic is, after all, the greatest of the pacific nations in resources, population and industrial capacity; the adherence of the American republic would, in effect, double the mass and powers of the projected league, and would so place it beyond all

hazard of defeat from without, or even of
serious outside opposition to its aims. Yet it
will not hold true that America is either disinterested or indispensable. To America, the
league is indispensable, as a refuge from
otherwise inevitable dangers ahead; single-
handed, America cannot defend itself, except at a prohibitive cost; whereas in co-
partnership with these others the national
defense becomes a virtually negligible matter. It is for America a choice between a
policy of extravagant armament with a
doubtful issue, and such abatement of national pretensions" [18] as would be needed.

4

Thorstein Veblen analyzed admirably the
fundamental implications of the First World
War. His analysis was neither understood
nor heeded: thus the dangerous situation of
the United States, and of the whole world,
which he had foreseen as a result of the possible recuperation of Germany and Japan,
has come about. But he could not foresee
that these two powers would prepare for

their new attempt not only by armaments, by economic adjustments and by military education of the people, but by a complete, or as it would be called now a total, and fundamental reinterpretation and reorientation of man's place in history. In recent German and Japanese history the will to power has probably played a greater role than in any other national history; yet there have been whole periods in which this will to power was far from being dominant. In the twenties of the present century, with the growth of democracy after the Allied victory in 1918 all over the earth, liberalism grew in strength in Germany and in Japan too. Japan then introduced universal suffrage; its Parliament became more and more representative; labor began to organize in trade unions; the universities came under the influence of liberal and socialist thought; the inclusion of Japan in the full stream of modern thought seemed imminent. The German Republic was in no way the weak, corrupt or contemptuous state which National-Socialist propaganda made it appear. There, as in

Vienna under the Social Democratic régime, much valuable progress was accomplished in many fields, and creative faculties set free produced an intensity of artistic and intellectual life witnessed in few other periods. The ultimate failure of liberalism in Japan and in Germany was not due to the Treaty of Versailles, but to the lack of creative vigor and courageous vision of democracy in the United States and in Great Britain in the twenties. This stagnation was not caused by economic reasons, for the United States, at least, was then advertised, to its own citizens and to the dazzled Europeans, as an economic miracle of prosperity. The roots of the stagnation lay in spiritual fatigue, in loss of faith, in an apparent exhaustion of the inspirational springs of democracy which expressed itself in short-sighted cynicism and in complacent pleasure-seeking. Personal egotism was matched by a national egotism which led to a policy of shirking of responsibilities and to an exaggerated and unfounded feeling of strength and security. The elections on December 14, 1918, in Great Britain and on November 4, 1920, in the United States expressed the transition from the "idealism" of the war to the "realism" of the post-war period. This weakening of democracy after its first great world-wide effort — an effort which had resulted not only in the transformation of conservative and monarchic Europe into a continent with predominantly republican and democratic constitutions but also in the awakening to active political life of the masses of Turkey and Egypt, India and China — gave those forces in Germany and Japan which loathed liberalism the opportunity for their triumph.

The underlying ideas of National Socialism and of Nipponism were hardly new in German or Japanese history. Though Japan received all her civilization from without, from China and Korea, Japanese history often displays the consciousness of the superiority of the Japanese race and of its resultant mission. At the end of the sixteenth century Hideyoshi Toyotomi decided to conquer the Celestial Empire, which then appeared identical with the world and civilization. He asked the Koreans to grant him right of passage and to support him. The way in which he addressed the ruler of the country sounds familiar in the twentieth century: "I will assemble a mighty host, and, invading the country of the great Ming (China), I will fill with the hoar-frost from my sword the whole sky over the four hundred provinces. Should I carry out this purpose, I hope that Korea will be my vanguard. Let her not fail to do so, for my friendship with your honorable country depends solely on your conduct when I lead my army against China." Characteristically, the Korean king answered: "What talk is this of our joining you against China? From the earliest times we have followed law and right. From within and from without, all lands are subject to China." [19] Hideyoshi did not succeed in his plans; the Seven Years War ended disastrously, though before his death the Japanese war-lord had sent his envoys as far as the Philippines and the Portuguese colony of Goa in India, demanding submission. In his letter to the Portuguese viceroy he promised that "after completing our heavenly mission of conquering China, we shall readily find a road by which to reach your country (India). Our war vessels and fighting men will accomplish the work entrusted to them regardless both of distance and the sort of warriors they may conquer." [20]

The failure of this venture at world conquest was followed by a long period of complete isolation. Toward its end, in the middle of the nineteenth century, the old spirit immediately reappeared. Then one of the heroes of modern Japan, Shōin Yoshida, expressed a determination, strangely reminding of similar attitudes on the part of National Socialist youth today who envisage only the alternative of complete triumph or of self-destruction involving the world's destruction: "I have a purpose and have determined to carry it out even though Mount Fuji crumbles and the rivers are exhausted." [21] Four years later, in 1858, Prime Minister Lord Hotta submitted a memorandum to the Emperor in which he suggested "laying a foundation for securing the hegemony over all

nations." In that memorandum he clearly
outlined the policy of the Empire eighty
years later: "Among the rulers of the world
at present, there is none so noble and illus-
trious as to command universal vassalage, or
who can make his virtuous influence felt
throughout the length and breadth of the
whole world. To have such a ruler over the
whole world is doubtless in conformity with
the Will of Heaven. . . . When our power
and national standing have come to be recognized, we should take the lead in punishing
the nation which may act contrary to the
principle of international interests; and in so
doing, we should join hands with the nations
whose principles may be found identical with
those of our country. An alliance thus formed
should also be directed towards protecting
harmless but powerless nations. Such a
policy could be nothing else but the enforcement of the power and authority deputed
(to us) by the Spirit of Heaven. Our national prestige and position thus ensured, the
nations of the world will come to look up to
our Emperor as the Great Ruler of all na-

tions and will come to follow our policy and submit themselves to our judgment." [22] Lord Hotta urged the Emperor to start the era of modernization in Japan and thus to seize the opportunity for realizing Japan's destiny. Eighty-three years later Lord Hotta's program, carried through after most careful preparations with a rare single-mindedness of purpose and national devotion, bore fruit before the eyes of the surprised world.

Thus Japan remained faithful to ancient traditions in her modern armor. But it was only after 1931, and not without some resistance in Japan proper — a resistance to which not only the many cases of imprisonment and torture of socialists, humanitarians, and intellectuals, but also the assassinations of high-placed Japanese bear witness — that what had been a tendency in Japanese history became an all-dominant force. The vehicle of this transformation — a transformation predetermined in the Japanese development but in no way its necessary outcome, and one which would not have taken place if the democratic nations had shown less national egotism and more creative imagination — was the imperial idea, summed up best by Shinkichi Uyesugi, professor of law at the Imperial University in Tokyo, in the words: "Our nationality is centered in one person, and it is our duty to develop and fulfil our destiny by observing our duty to the Throne, ultimately attaining the highest pinnacle of morality. We profess our faith, neither doubting nor fearing, and enjoy in it that perfect peace of mind which is the sum of happiness. Sacrificing ourselves, both in mind and body, with joy for the imperial idea, we promote it and obey it. This is the backbone of Japanese morality and the foundation of the national spirit. The standard of justice and injustice, of right and wrong, is to be fixed by the imperial will. All religions defer and yield pride of place to it. Philosophy holds good only when it is in conformity to the imperial will. That is the way and doctrine of the Japanese. We have but to obey, without doubt or demur; and we should do so not because the saints and sages of old so taught us, not because the learned have shown us that it is reasonable so to do, but because it is an imperial rescript." [23] This attitude of mystical devotion to a tribal deity or to the deification of the tribe would sound familiar in Germany to-day. It sounded incredible to the Western mind, which refused to take it seriously, as little as it took seriously National Socialism. But it cannot be said, either of the Japanese or of the German adherents of this new philosophy, that they did not publicly warn the civilized world. They spoke frankly and openly. When General Sadao Araki, then Minister of War, published in the Army Club's Monthly an article on the Imperial Principle of the Japanese Nation, this article was translated into English in a Japanese journal. It announced to the world that "the Imperial Principle, which is the aggregate of the true spirit underlying the very foundation of the State and the national ideal of the Japanese, *is, by its nature, a thing that must be propagated over the seven seas and extended over the five continents. Anything that may hinder its progress must be done away with even by the use of force. . . . It is no idle boast to declare herewith that if there is anything that would dare obstruct the way for the propagation of Japan's mission of peace, the Japanese would be ready, in spirit at least, to make away with it."* [24]

In a recent publication the Japanese Department of Education declared that Japan "is a divine country ruled over by the Son of Heaven who is manifest God." [25] In April 1938, in a definite attempt to stamp out liberalism in education, Ishii Tsutomu of the Department of Education wrote: "The power for living and growing shows itself perfectly in Japan only. That is why the national structure of Japan is incomparable. In this meaning, Japan has a style of national structure in which people live harmoniously as though they were in one family. And the world must follow this way of living of Japan and move according to this national structure, and it is the ultimate way of living given to mankind by god. After all, the world will follow the model of Japan, in spite of their will, because Japan is the one representation of the one power which flows through all phenomena of the universe. This power of the universe will never end and will become more clear to the peoples of the world through the Japanese national structure and moral spirit. It is most important that the literature, culture and science of Japan be built upon this spiritual basis." [26] As fantastic as this sounds, it nevertheless sounds familiar to those acquainted with recent German writings.

The similarity goes even deeper. As National Socialists reject Christianity and Western rational civilization as something alien to the German spirit, as something imposed upon it, and demand the purification and the reassertion of the original German spirit, so the Japanese thinkers reject not only Western rational civilization, but Chinese civilization and Buddhism, which they regard as foreign to the original Japanese tradition. Norinaga Motoori, who lived in the second half of the eighteenth century, in a most interesting and suggestive polemic against the Chinese ethics accepted in Japan tried to prove their relativity in a way which again brings to mind contemporary attacks against universal and rational ethical standards. "If what the Chinese call Benevolence, Righteousness, Propriety, Retiringness, Filial Piety, Brotherly Love, Fidelity, and Truth really constituted the duty of man, they would be so recognized and practised without any teaching, but as they were invented by the so-called Holy Men as instruments for ruling a viciously inclined population, it became necessary to insist on more than the actual duty of man. Consequently, although plenty of men profess these doctrines, the number of those who practised them is very small. Violations of this teaching were attributed to human lusts. As human lusts are a part of man's nature, they must be a part of the harmony of the universe, and cannot be wrong. . . . To have acquired the knowledge that there is no ethics to be learned and practised is really to have learned to practise the way of the Gods." [27] With this denial of universal and rational ethics, with this interpretation of the ethics as an invention of priests and thus not binding upon superior men, who may follow their lusts, comes the familiar insistence upon the Japanese being these superior men. Motoori's disciple Atsutane Hirata, who like his teacher worked to evolve a living faith in the ancient Shinto, drew this conclusion without hesitation in the beginning of the nineteenth century. "Between the Japanese people and other nations of the world, there is a difference of kind rather than of degree. It was not out of vainglory that the inhabitants of this country called it the land of the gods. The gods who created all countries were all born in Japan." Hirata prefaced this statement of truth with the lament "that so much ignorance should prevail as to the evidence" of this fundamental doctrine.[28] This ignorance prevailed, not only in the rest of the world but even to some extent in Japan until very recently. At present [29] the Japanese have successfully indoctrinated their youth with this fundamental doctrine, have silenced dissentient voices, and have set out to "diffuse this truth through the globe and make it accepted by everyone." In this respect again the situation completely resembles that in Germany. The total and uncompromising rejection of rational and universal ethics, the return to the ancient gods of the tribe have been used in both cases for the same purpose, to make the nation the most perfect instrument for world conquest, to imbue it with a death-defying will to fulfill its mission, whether upon the ruins of the world or upon a pyre of its own happiness and comfort.

Like Japan, the Germans have been famous from antiquity, and deservedly so, for their martial spirit and their outstanding discipline. The sense of subordination, the lack of personal independence, was no gift of Prussia. It is true that the inheritance of the Teutonic Knights, the geographic and social peculiarities of the land east of the Elbe, and the genius of Frederick William I and of Frederick II of the house of Hohenzollern have gone far to identify Prussia with Sparta. But Goethe did not think of Prussia when in his conversation with Eckermann on March 12, 1828, he praised the liberty of English-

men, "das Glück der persönlichen Freiheit,"
which endows them with uprightness, while
in Germany every little boy grows up under the strict eye of the police. Whenever
he tries to feel himself at liberty, "sogleich
ist die Polizei da, es zu verbieten." It may
be that this lack of personal liberty in social
and political life induced the daring exploits
of intellectual liberty and irresponsibility in
which many German thinkers indulged, and
that the absence of the "Glück der persönlichen Freiheit" found its compensation in
far-flung dreams of disciplined power and
conquest. Only a very few years after Friedrich List drew up — amidst a people still apparently composed of dreamy poets and quiet
thinkers — the first clearly coördinated polit-
ico-economic power program for national
aggrandizement and German *Weltgeltung*,
Ferdinand Kürnberger published in 1855 his
novel, *Der Amerikamüde*, a cultural picture
of the United States. In this thoughtful but
angry book, one of the enthusiasts for the
coming unity and freedom of Germany en-
visages the future of the United States, of

the German element in it, and of himself as one who will work for this future: "What the German farmers in Pennsylvania were able to do unconsciously, to preserve German life through a whole century so strongly that even today whole communities of theirs do not understand one English word, should I be less able to do, with my enthusiastic consciousness of German kind and culture? I am not afraid of it. No, I shall last, a German in Yankeedom, and the fall which I foresee for this racial mixture can worry me as little as we are worried by the fate of a goat which has nursed Jupiter to strength. May it then happen, as these pages dare to prophesy, we shall not perish in the civil wars of the Union. Germany will send her fleet, and will know how to protect her German province, Pennsylvania. What do I say: Pennsylvania? The whole of North America will become German, for our immigration leans upon a powerful mother country, as Yankee England leaned upon old England. But what do I say: the whole of North America? The whole world will become German, for Germany's rise will mean England's decline, as Holland declined before England, and all English colonies will then fall to the Germans; the guards of culture on the whole earth will be changed and their posts will be occupied by German troops. Germany awakens, and no people on earth can keep its old rank, for all live thanks to the German sleep and perish with German awakening." [30]

Extravagant dreams such as this were not shared by the overwhelming majority of more sober thinking Germans. But the underlying sentiments were expressed, in a more disciplined way, by some other German thinkers, leaders, and dreamers. With the miraculous successes of the Prussian army and of Bismarck's policy their number grew. Germany perfected step by step her instrumentalities for power politics on a world wide scale. In the First World War she came within reach of her goal. Though numerically and in resources much inferior to her enemies, she far surpassed them by the range of her preparations and by her intelligent and thorough coordination of the different branches of life for the purpose of the war.

When Germany lost the war many Germans believed that it was due to the insufficient integration of the masses into the German national purpose, to the insufficient mobilization of all the resources of the people and the land. Chancellor Hitler did not raise any new goals before the German nation; he made what had been the conscious aim of a small minority into a dream shared by the people; he prepared the whole German nation, all its classes and especially its masses, for a total mobilization which would no longer allow internal dissensions, doubts, class and party antagonism, to weaken the German war effort. The school of thought that he represented was convinced that Germany had not been defeated by the arms of the enemy from without, but by the strength of liberalism, socialism, pacifism, by all that which is known as Western thought, Christianity, or humanitarianism, from within. For that purpose he preached the new concept of a total, universal, absolute war, as something determining everything everywhere and at every time,[31] the transformation of man into a warrior or rather into an indus-

trial-military soldier-worker. To achieve this
end it was not sufficient to combat and eradi-
cate all the feelings of humanitarianism, of
charity, of sympathy with everything human,
of a common bond with other nations or with
non-Germans, all regard for their possible
rights. What was needed was not only a
streamlined and vulgarized Nietzscheanism,[32]
but an absolute hostility against everything
without, an absolute cohesion within. "If the
German nation," Hitler wrote, "had achieved
in its historical development that herd-like
unity . . . , then the German Reich would
be today master of the globe." [33] Chancellor
Hitler set himself the task of eradicating in
Germany not only all feeling of human brotherhood and of humanity but also all feeling
of individuality and individualism, thus to
weld the Germans into one uniform body
with one aim and one mind, and to make the
German Reich master of the globe.

This spiritual transformation of Germany
was regarded from the beginning not as a
national but as a world phenomenon; the
German crisis appeared to the Germans

themselves as the heightened expression, the exemplary realization and solution of a world crisis. For "Germany's position is a central one. She is a focus of all political, economic, and intellectual problems. If the world wants salvation, and so far as it deserves salvation, Germany will be able to express whatever this revolutionized world can hope to salvage." [34] Thus the German plan of mastery of the globe merged with the world crisis and world revolution. From there it gained its appeal to all those millions in all countries and all races who responded to the crisis and its challenge as the National Socialists did. By its revolutionary crisis-element it was able to exploit to its own profit all the weaknesses, half-heartedness, and hypocrisies which the crisis had revealed with frightening clarity in the mental and moral texture of those whom National Socialism had set out to destroy everywhere — pacifists and nationalists, conservative business men and socialists, Christians and liberals. They all were blind to the depths of the crisis of which the National Socialists were only too clearly aware. On account of their blindness they continued the polite and comfortable though most dangerous fiction that the German and Japanese governments were normal governments within the common framework of the accepted values of human civilization, while it was the very essence of the crisis, partly expressing it and partly driving it forward to its catastrophic conclusion, that in the thirties of the twentieth century these governments of two ancient and powerful nations, endowed with greatest intellectual abilities and eminent virtues, had in reality abandoned the framework of common civilized values and began a relentless campaign to destroy it.

5

The great strength of National Socialism, its aggressive and missionary ardor, its appeal and fascination, derive from its full awareness of the weight and implications of the crisis. National Socialism, partly a result of the crisis, represents its most unmistakable and terrifying manifestation and its most potent agency. Its victorious expansion today, but also the determined resistance it has lately encountered, are proof that the crisis has arrived at its climax, at the crossroads between recovery and ruin. The hour of decision has arrived: Germany and Japan have foreseen it for a long time and have prepared for it. They have recognized the world-wide character of the crisis and its fundamental and absolute challenge to civilization. They had vision and courage, and they put these virtues into the service of total corruption. The democracies, much less corrupted, had neither vision nor courage. The crisis was so great and so unique, so unprecedented in its extent and its intensity, its consequences so unimaginable and terrifying, that it transcended the grasp of the common man. Man can grasp a crisis limited in space and object, he can understand a war for circumscribed goals, for certain territories or economic resources. He can only with difficulty, with a supreme effort, imagine a crisis or a war in which everything is at stake, where there exists no limit to the immediate effects of the war but the confines of the globe and the complete revaluation of all values. This fact explains the fright and the apathy so characteristic of the masses in this crisis and this war. For everything is at stake, the six continents and the seven seas, the control of the skies and of the resources beneath the soil, and all civilization. Germany and Japan will be defeated and the crisis overcome only when the peoples in danger of falling as victims have become fully conscious of the character of the crisis and its implications.

All civilization is at stake. This is far more than a war between Christianity and paganism. Hitler may have broken completely with Christianity; the Japanese warlords may have never been touched by it: against them are fighting not only Christians but Buddhists and Confucians, Hindus and Mohammedans, agnostics and atheists also. All of them are part of the civilization endangered. For all civilization is a restraint imposed by divine or rational law upon the instincts of man; it is an advance beyond tribalism and the deification of the tribe as the only focal point of the integration and meaning of all human life, to the recognition of the dignity of every individual independent of any tribal organization, and of the common kind and destiny of humanity, above, and far more important than, all its divisions. The evolution beyond tribalism, the recognition of the worth of the individual and of the oneness of mankind, of standards of ethics and truth common to and binding upon all men, the majesty of law founded upon justice, these are the foundations of civilization which cannot be denied without civilization itself crumbling. They can be betrayed again and again in individual cases and falsified by half-heartedness or hypocrisy; as long as they are not radically denied and rejected, as long as they are violated with a bad conscience or at least an uncertain feeling of guilt, as long as lip service is being paid to them, civilization still survives. What has happened in our days, an unprecedented and almost unimaginable fact, is a conscious rejection of the foundations of civilization, a *return* to tribalism, a reversal of the whole trend of history.

All civilized human relations are based
upon a reciprocity which may be founded
either upon the belief that man is created in
the image of God (and all men without ex-
ception are descended from one human cou-
ple, have survived in the same ark and have
witnessed the same rainbow) or upon the belief that all men participate in common sense
and reason. This reciprocity is meant when
Jesus says that the law and the prophets are
contained in the command "All things what-
soever ye would that men should do to you,
do ye even also unto them"; it is meant by the
categorical imperative and Kant's injunction
to treat man always as an end and not as a
means. All justice which deserves the name
is based upon reciprocity, and this means,
upon equality. Reciprocity and equality not
only are the indispensable pillars of justice;
they also create that tie of sympathy with
everything human, that feeling of compassion and respect in which, above all differences of climate and epoch, the inscriptions
of the Buddhist emperor Asoka, the *homo
homini res sacra* of the Roman Stoic, and

Albert Schweitzer's hospital in Lambarene all participate. In the fundamental concepts of civilization there is nothing new: they have been stated again and again, at least as far back as the sixth century B.C. This *philosophia perennis* is expressed in different ages in different ways, but the content is one — whether Antigone appeals to "the immutable unwritten laws of Heaven," or Jefferson to the Laws of Nature and self-evident truths. The concept of the oneness of mankind was proclaimed by Amos when he hurled at the Israelites, self-confident with tribal pride, the words, "Are ye not as children of the Ethiopians unto me, O children of Israel? Have not I brought up Israel out of the land of Egypt?" On this miraculous feat of history Israel's tribal pride was based; but the prophet went on, destroying forever the exclusiveness of Israel's privilege — "and the Philistines from Caphtor, and the Syrians from Kir?" From that recognition of the oneness of mankind and of the equal care bestowed by God upon all peoples there is only one step to the blessing spoken by Isaiah over all nations, foe and friend alike: "Blessed be Egypt, my people, and Assyria, the work of my hands, and Israel, my inheritance."

There is no greater contrast thinkable than that between the Prophets and the spokesmen of the Germans and the Japanese, for the Prophets did not flatter their people and its instincts, its supposedly exceptional gifts and mission, they condemned it in words of unsurpassed violence because they measured its life and actions by standards of absolute justice. They spoke not of power and glory but of repentance and punishment. To them all peoples were equal before God; so were all individuals, the poor as well as the rich, the meek and powerless as well as the powerful. The Prophets were above all concerned with the poor and uncomely ones on earth, with those who are despised and rejected of men, people of sorrows and acquainted with grief. There is still a far step from this point to the modern rights of man, but the rights of man repose on this foundation, to which appeal has been made again and ever again throughout history. For though the rights of man were only formulated in the eighteenth century, their roots are in the Prophets and in the Stoa; they are the inheritance of the whole course of civilization. "Medieval doctrine was already filled with the thought of the inborn and indestructible rights of the individual. . . . Through it all runs the thought of the absolute and imperishable value of the individual. . . . That every individual by virtue of his eternal destination is at the core somewhat holy and indestructible even in relation to the highest power; that the smallest part has a value of its own, and not merely because it is part of a whole; that every man is to be regarded never as a mere instrument, but also as an end; all this is not merely suggested, but is more or less clearly expressed" in medieval doctrine.[35] The Declaration of the Rights of Man was not the expression of abstract principles formulated in the eighteenth century and useful or valid only in the social and political conditions of the epoch; it was the fruition of the long labor of the human mind, the only practical foundation upon which civilized life can be built anywhere.[36]

Liberty and equality, peace and justice, are not meaningless abstractions or "ideologies" covering up the needs or desires of certain classes or nations or groups. Their validity is not impaired by the fact that they can be found in history only in a relative and imperfect form. All four of them are closely interrelated, but at the same time conflicting in their realization. All justice is based upon equality,[37] but no justice can be exercised without some limitations on liberty. Liberty demands freedom from forceful restraint, and that means peace, but no peace can be maintained, and therefore no liberty, without application of force — without the readiness to apply all necessary force, though only that strictly necessary. Liberty and equality, peace and justice are not dogmas, they are directions. A utopianism which would be satisfied only with absolute liberty or absolute equality is as dangerous to real liberty and equality, peace and justice, as the cynicism which in the wake of the nineteenth-cen-

in our time is endangered not on account of certain political or economic failures but because something more fundamental is threatened, the sense and conviction of direction. "Perhaps not the actual content of Natural Law, but the belief that the Natural Law does exist, not any actually recognized natural rights, but the admission that there are natural rights, is the important fact. The greatest significance of these ideas may lie, not in what they did, but in what they prevented being done." [38] National Socialism (in its German and its Japanese form) [39] has drawn its immense strength from its full realization of the fundamental crisis of civilization. It felt the loss of the sense of direction; it decided to reverse the trend. That was one possible way out of the crisis: the complete ruin of civilization. Thus it did everything to make the crisis more acute. The democratic peoples, though deeply affected by the crisis, did not realize its fundamental character. They continued to drift in the old direction but there was no drive in the drift; the goal seemed lost, the vigor gone. They

had neither the vision nor the strength to resolve upon the other possible way out of the
crisis: the recovery of civilization.

Thus they were entirely unprepared, not
only in their armaments but also in their
minds, for the onslaught of National Socialism. By their unpreparedness they precip-
itated the open outbreak of the crisis. The
National Socialists, not only those of Germany and Japan, saw themselves already on
the verge of triumph. They surveyed the
scene around them: the apathy and the refusal to face the reality and to act courageously, the blindness and egotism of isolationism, the degradation of pacifism,[40] all the
"logical" and "ethical" subterfuges presented
by the fertility of the human mind. One of
these was the ripest fruit of relativism, the
"conviction" that there was no difference between the inconsistencies and inadequacies
of democracy on the one hand and the rejection of all liberty and equality in National
Socialism on the other hand — as if a sick
civilization were the same as a dead civilization. That there was a hope and a promise

to be saved, a hope and a promise by which men had worked their way up painfully and under much labor for more than two thousand years, was denied. And so the wave of the future rolled along to engulf the whole earth and all civilization that had been the work of the past. And there was no ark in sight.

6

In May 1940 the world-wide victory of National Socialism seemed assured through the refusal of the other peoples to understand the issues involved. Even the peoples fighting in the war against National Socialism did not know what they were fighting against or what they were fighting for. They believed they were fighting a normal war, like all their former wars. They had known wars: if they ended adversely, they might result in some loss of territory or of economic opportunities, in some shift of power or of wealth, but other things would be left much as they had been. The National Socialists knew clearly what they were fighting against

and what they were fighting for; they knew
that the battle was engaged for the highest
stakes — for unprecedented, almost unimaginable, consequences — and they had prepared for it. Their victory seemed to be
made easy by the new International which
the crisis had produced as one of its most
characteristic symptoms, the world-wide international of isolationists of all nationalities
— who all, whatever their conflicting national
interests and view-points, disagreements and
hatreds, repeated the same arguments with
local variations. The isolationists in Poland
and in France, in Great Britain and in Ireland, in Norway and in the United States,
in Canada and in the Argentine, accepted,
sometimes simultaneously and sometimes one
after the other, the successive clichés which
were to explain away the fascist pattern of
world conquest and to smooth the way for
it. National Socialist propaganda did not in-
tend to convert most of these isolationists to
National Socialism, but to weaken the possibility of timely and resolute resistance. In
that it succeeded.

Each nation believed itself secure by reason of its special national conditions and the geographical situation which guaranteed its independent destiny. Each wished to keep its own house in order and to beware of knight errantry abroad, arguing that the cause of peace could never be promoted by extending the conflict (though how the cause of peace could be served by the piecemeal resistance of each attacked nation was never explained). Complacent dreams befogged the issues: Germany and Japan would be unable to survive financially and economically the strain of war; their armies would be too deeply engaged in far-off areas to direct their attention to other areas whose safety would thus be guaranteed by the misery of some other part of mankind; a defensive strategy would miraculously guarantee victory. Dreams like these were seriously debated as realities for many years, until a complacent dream world found itself face to face with the events of May 1940. That month marked the climax of the crisis. It was epitomized in the fall of France; the fall and not the defeat. France had been defeated before, but she had never betrayed herself. Not that the military débâcle of France was due primarily to treachery. It was due to the woeful incompetence of the generals who in June 1940, by Pétain's coup d'état, tried to save themselves from facing the responsibility for the defeat. The betrayal came after the military collapse. Pilsudski has said that "to be vanquished and yet not surrender, that is the greatest victory." In the Second World War the Poles and the Serbs, the Norwegians and the Dutch have been vanquished, yet they have not surrendered. On previous occasions the French have shown a similar spirit. Like Pétain's France, the Third Republic was born in a defeat. But how differently, how heroically did the Frenchmen of Gambetta react as compared with the Frenchmen of Pétain! The Crown Prince of Germany wrote at the German Headquarters in Versailles on the 31st of December, 1870: "The assumption seemed justified that France after the battle of Sedan was utterly crushed, that the nation was broken in morale and incapable of further resistance, that Paris itself, the capital city of pleasure, would instantly capitulate 'if it were only a single day without strawberries.' But in all points the exact contrary was manifested. The French people day by day rose higher from its degradation; it seemed as though the downfall of its former Government had given it back strength, courage and honour, as though Generals and Statesmen it had hitherto so sorely lacked had sprung up again to win back what was lost. Men like Gambetta and Trochu were not wanting at any rate in boldness and capacity. And on all sides we see new armies, made up of volunteers, arise out of nothing; never, it is true, have these become a force of trained soldiers, but they are often much superior to us in numbers, and day by day gain in efficiency and fighting capability, to vanquish which will cost us heavy sacrifices. But it is the capital which holds us at bay before her gates and puts our endurance to the severest proof." [41] In June 1940, after another battle of Sedan, Paris surrendered without even the slightest show of resistance, the only such case of ignominious self-abandonment of a great city in this war.

The military defeat of France became a spiritual triumph for National Socialism. For France surrendered to National Socialism. What had happened in Spain a few years before — only that in Spain it had happened against the glorious and heroic resistance of the Spanish people — happened now in France: a group of fascist reactionaries, full of hatred against democracy, the dignity of the individual, and the equality of all, seized power. In Spain the fascist revolt against liberalism had happened first, and only then German help arrived to put it in the saddle; in France the Germans arrived first, and in their wake the fascist generals and politicians found the opportunity to seize power and to destroy with German help the French Republic. They took their revenge for 1789, for the Dreyfus affair, and for the reassertion of democracy in France in May 1936. Marshal Pétain's surrender, born not out of military necessity but out of a hatred for democracy greater than the desire to avert a German victory, helped Germany more than any other single act in this war. If France had resisted as the Netherlands and Norway resisted, the war would have taken an entirely different turn. The English and French navies and armies would have controlled the Mediterranean, would have easily defeated Italy and prevented the conquest of the Balkans. Northwestern Africa and Indo-China would have been saved, the Japanese march towards the Philippines and the Dutch East Indies made much more difficult, the German threat to the Western Hemisphere removed.

Even more important than the strategic implications of the betrayal were its moral consequences. For France was not a country like other European countries; for two hundred years she had been the guardian of human liberties on the continent of Europe. Liberals in Spain and in Russia, in Greece and in Denmark, in Italy and in Germany, had looked to France for inspiration and for guidance. For every liberal on the European

continent and in the Near East France was
a second home, a citadel of light, sacred
through the generous dreams of 1789 and
1848, the ideal of the equality of all men, the
incessant struggle for justice, for greater tolerance, for more enlightenment. That ven-
eration for France remained untouched by
the vicissitudes of war. This time it was different. Paris had been invaded before; it
had never fallen. And in times of defeat
and crisis the love for France of all her millions of friends and grateful disciples was not
diminished, but grew. They did not measure
France by success, but by her exemplary
loyalty to her great message of liberty, equality, fraternity. The ship of France carried
the hope of the continent. *Fluctuat nec
mergitur.* Now it was submerged in the mud,
abandoned in panic and irresolution, in betrayal and defeatism, by its own crew. War-
saw was in ruins, but the spirit of the Polish
people was unbroken. Norway and Serbia
were occupied all over their territories, but
their people were fighting on. In France
there was even a "free" France with its gov-

ernment on metropolitan soil, but this "free"
France abandoned the struggle for liberty,
for democracy, for the French traditions of
1789, paid homage to the National Socialist
idea, and helped to defile the great memories
of France as ferociously as the National Socialists denounced them. The Germans could
only rejoice when they heard that all the
abuse which they had heaped upon the
French people and its state for so many years
was now repeated eagerly by the new rulers
of France. As if the Third Republic had not
written some of the most glorious pages of
French history! It had created a French Empire in place of that lost by the French monarchy; it had given full play to all the creative
faculties of the French genius; it had facil-
itated a flowering of letters and arts which
made Paris the capital of painters and of
writers; it had made possible a renaissance
of Catholic thought, in Bergson and Bloy,
in Péguy and Claudel, in Bernanos and Maritain, without parallel in the contemporary
world. True, the Republic had known cases
of gross corruption, and its citizens had not

always lived up to standards of civic virtue, but that was nothing peculiar to the regime. Corruption and lack of civic virtue had been greater under the monarchy, under Louis XV, and in the German and Italian principalities of the eighteenth century; they throve most in the countries least touched by the spirit of the French Revolution. In spite of a widespread legend, the new order created by the victory of the ideas of 1776 and 1789 has uprooted the inveterate corruption of the old order of authority and inequality; in democracies corruption has grown infinitely less, and has been more energetically and publicly condemned and combatted.

The fall of France had a symbolic portent. The citadel of liberty had fallen, had surrendered to the triumphant enemy. Chancellor Hitler's armies were now spread from the northern tip of Norway to the Bay of Biscay, facing a practically unarmed Britain: the greatest and best prepared military machine of all ages, with an air force of unprecedented strength, challenged the small island where few preparations had been made to meet the challenge of which it had been believed that it could not happen. Chancellor Hitler was certain that England would fall. With her fall world dominion would be his. The Western Hemisphere was practically unarmed and therefore indefensible; simultaneous moves in the Atlantic and in the Pacific would have quickly brought more than one strategic vantage point in the Americas under German and Japanese control. But military invasion might have been unnecessary. The breakdown of democracy, the world-wide triumph of totalitarianism were taken for granted. Fascism was proclaimed the wave of the future which could and should not be resisted. In May 1940 when the fall of England seemed imminent and, with the possible elimination of the British fleet, the oceans were broad highways to many landing places in the two vast western continents for the defense of which neither armies nor air forces existed, at the moment when democracy seemed lost and the possible tragic consequences began to dawn upon the Americans, they were admonished to "stop this hysterical chatter of calamity and invasion. Nobody wants to attack us and no one is in a position to do it." That was in May 1940, the greatest depression that the cause of human freedom and dignity ever has touched.

In this unforgettable world-hour when the destiny of mankind was in the balance as never before, and the scales seemed to the National Socialists of all lands irresistibly loaded in favor of the triumphantly proclaimed wave of the future, the moral resolve of the British people alone, not the nonexistent might of British or American arms, stood between Chancellor Hitler and the full realization of his dream of a National Socialist world. The British people, after twenty years of the apparently easy life of isolation and peace, for a long time had been unable to understand the challenge, though probably more individuals in all classes were ready to respond to the challenge there than in any other country. What neither Chancellor Hitler nor Signor Mussolini — who heroically had entered the war in the moment when he believed that it was all over —

neither Marshal Pétain nor the friends of the wave of the future in other lands, had thought possible, happened. The English people decided to resist, and by this response to the challenge broke the wave of the future. Democracy had started on the road to recovery, had begun to gather faith, had found itself again, and words which had become anemic shadows of a great past regained some of their old meaning and dignity.

The resolve of the British people found a voice in Winston Churchill. With all his personal and national limitations, he grew for one fleeting hour of history — but one of its supreme and decisive hours — into the embodiment of the will of his people in a sudden surge of moral regeneration. This typical Englishman focused the rising hope in the hearts of countless millions in all countries and races whose vision he lighted and whose courage he lifted. In the dark hour when he became Prime Minister, on May 13, 1940, for the first time, after all the unreality, hypocrisy and half-heartedness of twenty long years, a new clarity and determination rang forth in unforgettable words. "I have nothing to offer but blood, toil, tears, and sweat." "To wage war against the monstrous tyranny, never surpassed in the dark, lamentable catalogue of human crime, that is our policy." "Without victory there is no survival." Until, in the most tragic and portentous hour, when France had sued for an armistice, a brief message of seven short sentences contained the proud and simple words: "We have become the sole champions now in arms to defend the world cause." Yet Churchill was only the voice. If there ever was a people's war since the great revolutionary wars, this war which Chancellor Hitler and his friends tried to stigmatize as poor Mr. Chamberlain's war, has been a people's war. With all their many human and all-too-human limitations and iniquities, the English people will be remembered as much for their fortitude in upholding the world cause of liberty and human dignity in 1940 as for their leadership in the seventeenth century.[42]

Chancellor Hitler and his friends, in a strange perversion of facts, have claimed that

Great Britain abandoned France. The truth is not only that France abandoned Great Britain instead of fighting on as so many other nations did, but that Great Britain took, a few days before France's surrender, an unprecedented step which was animated by the vision which alone can overcome this crisis and assure recovery. The proposal submitted by Great Britain brushed away with a daring courage all the accumulated distrust and memories of friction of many centuries. It set the path to a rebuilding of mankind as no other single step has done. It was not the wishful program of a private association or of isolated intellectuals. It was the offer of a government in power, speaking authoritatively for the whole nation. It suggested the fusion of the most ancient and memorable realms of Great Britain and France, the center of so many of the greatest memories of mankind, in a new union. There is no single official document which shows a greater understanding of the nature of the challenge and of the right kind of response. If it had been accepted, there in the midst of the war, a new beginning would have been made. Not only the strategic and immediate consequences, but the ultimate effect upon the peace of mankind would have been incalculable. The proposed declaration of union, submitted by the British government to the French government in June 1940, read:

"At this most fateful moment in the history of the modern world the governments of the United Kingdom and the French Republic make this declaration of indissoluble union and unyielding resolution in their common defence of justice and freedom, against subjection to a system which reduces mankind to a life of robots and slaves. The two Governments declare that France and Great Britain shall no longer be two nations but one Franco-British Union. The constitution of the Union will provide for joint organs of defence, foreign, financial, and economic policies. Every citizen of France will enjoy immediately citizenship of Great Britain, every British subject will become a citizen of France. Both countries will share responsibility for the repair of the devastation of war, wherever it occurs in their territories, and the resources of both shall be equally, and as one, applied to that purpose. During the war there shall be a single war Cabinet, and all the forces of Britain and France, whether on land, sea, or in the air, will be placed under its direction. It will govern from wherever it best can. The two Parliaments will be formally associated. The nations of the British Empire are already forming new armies. France will keep her available forces in the field, on the sea, and in the air. The Union appeals to the United States to fortify the economic resources of the Allies and to bring her powerful material aid to the common cause. The Union will concentrate its whole energy against the power of the enemy no matter where the battle may be. And thus we shall conquer."

It was only with a very slight majority that the French Cabinet rejected the Union. If it had accepted, democracy would have won the battle. The Union would have become a rallying point. It was the spiritual defeatism in France, shared by so many circles in the

United States, which decided the issue. Too deeply had the mind been corroded by the false beliefs that democracy cannot survive war, that all resistance is futile, by the uncritical acceptance of the fascist (and communist) disparagements of democracy through absolutizing its relative defects and imperfections, by the fictitious alternative of fascism or communism and the ensuing fear of communism. Even the friends of democracy spoke apologetically and tried to prove that after all democracy was not so inefficient and that there might be something worth while in the dignity of man, in the equality of all men, and in the promise of freedom and peace embedded in the message of democracy. In such an intellectual and moral climate the most fantastic almost became reality and the end of civilization seemed in sight. Never before had mankind been so ready to betray itself and its millenary hopes.

In this very hour the recovery began. It was not more than an uncertain and groping beginning, still exposed to innumerable mortal dangers. But the first light of hope had appeared, in the midst of destruction and ruin. It was the war, not the years of peace, which brought about the regeneration of the British people. Chancellor Hitler and his fellow admirers of efficiency and machines, of arms and might, not only did not foresee it; they could not understand it. What had taken place was a spiritual awakening, a new vision of the mind, a new courage of the heart. It was not confined to Great Britain; it has happened in Spain and in China, in Serbia and in Poland.[43] It slowly gained momentum; the wave of the future broke itself at the wall, not of Maginot Lines of concrete or water, but at the wall of human minds. The myth of inevitability, whether based upon a crude application of superficial and spurious sociological laws or upon mystical fervor, had shown its emptiness. And while the often-admired efficiency of Mussolini's fascism, the father of a world-wide offspring of lawlessness and violence, broke down under the resistance of the small and poorly equipped Greek army and the minute British forces in Africa, the mother of "decadent" parliamentarism rose to the occasion and weathered the unprecedented storm with dignity and distinction. The summer of 1940 gave to the freedom of man a new, and it may be the last, chance to overcome the crisis.

7

In his Christmas message to the German fighting forces Marshal Walther von Brauchitsch, in reviewing the events of 1940 from his headquarters somewhere on the English Channel, said: "A great and proud year has passed. Once again I speak to you under a Christmas tree. The last time was before the Maginot Line which was supposed to protect France and could not. Today we are before a sea wall that will protect England only so long as it suits us. England now stands alone. So we have only one more task to do: beat this last and most embittered opponent to the ground and win the peace." [44] One year later England was not standing alone any more. It was Chancellor Hitler himself who by his deliberate actions had given new and powerful allies to Great Britain, countries unwilling to understand the crisis and to act out of vision and courage until they were forced into action by attacks from outside which compelled them to abandon their isolationist policies: the Soviet Union and the United States. By the end of 1941 the global character of the war and the total character of the crisis had become manifest, so unmistakably had the signs been written by German and Japanese actions over all continents and all seas. Not only Great Britain, but also the Soviet Union and the United States were now fighting for their survival; the German and the Japanese warlords were confident that victory would take them to London, Moscow and Washington. Supported by American and British complacency, — a feeling of false strength, based upon wealth, upon the underestimation of the enemy, and the deeply rooted belief that it could not happen here, — the Japanese looked forward to fulfilling their mission in the vast expanse from the eastern shores of Africa to the western shores of the Western Hemisphere while Germany hoped to join hands with Japan across Russia or across the Middle East, thus to complete the encirclement of America and ensure the domination of the globe by the military strength of the two nations who believed themselves chosen by blood and destiny to rule the world.[45]

As the world-wide pattern of conquest became manifest, the understanding of the mental attitude behind National Socialism and the Japanese imperial myth grew. Their apotheosis of barbarism as the iron logic of nature, the inner meaning of history, and the inevitable wave of the future was recognized as a mortal challenge to the most different and even opposite schools of thought. Alfred Rosenberg's plans for a National Reich Church as Germany's only admitted religious organization, based upon *Mein Kampf* as "the purest ethnic morals under which the German people must live," threatened not only Christianity, but humanity.[46] An anonymous book, *Gott und Volk*, widely and officially circulated in Germany in the fall of 1941, accused the Church of having degenerated into a restraining impediment instead of moulding mankind into a cleaner, higher-striving race. "Finally, the Führer and his movement have come, decried as heretic, to perceive and form true divine will. A thousand bonds tie us to the Christian belief. But one blow will make us free. To make Germans strong and ripe for the step is our task, our holiest obligation. German faith won't dictate to anyone his relationship to God. Everyone seeks his own way. But no one seeks it in Rome or Jerusalem. Germany is our holy land. It will be our religion. We want faith which flames out of the depths of German nature and out of German hearts."[47] This declaration of war against Christianity was a declaration of war against all civilization in the name of a purely tribal morale. This morale may produce the highest forms of devotion and sacrifice in the service of a cause which totally rejects all universal ethics and thus is void of any norm with meaning for mankind. It represents absolute personal devotion to extreme ethical relativism.[48] No compromise and no understanding are possi-

ble between this tribal morale and human
civilization. With all their differences, British Protestant liberalism, Roman Catholic
conservatism, and Russian communism are
heirs to the common tradition of civilization.
In varying interpretations they believe in the
oneness of mankind and in the worth of every
individual.[49] The trends of thought and social forces represented by Winston Churchill
and those which found in Lenin and Stalin
their symbol were bitterly hostile in the recent past. Roman Catholic conservatism regarded Anglo-Saxon Protestant liberalism as
the destroyer of Spanish world leadership
from the first blow in 1588 to the final stroke
in 1898. Nor was any love lost between the
Roman Catholic Church and Russian communism. Nevertheless, the struggle for survival against a common enemy who with an
unprecedented daring rejects for the first
time the foundations of all civilization has
driven the most opposite forces into a common defensive.

They all have begun to understand that
they are passing through the gravest crisis

of history. The administrative board of the National Catholic Welfare Conference published on November 17, 1941, a statement on the crisis of Christianity by the Catholic bishops of the United States which began, "Christianity faces today its most serious crisis since the Church came out of the Catacombs." It recalled that Pope Pius XI had with "prophetic vision" declared that National Socialist "machinations, from the beginning, had no other aims than a war of extermination." The Pope had branded the "Nazi oppressors of the Church in Germany" as "the nullifiers and destroyers of the Christian West." In his broadcast on Christmas Eve 1941 Pope Pius XII reaffirmed his predecessor's opposition to the new order of tribalism. He opposed to it a new order based upon universal ethics which "must be founded on that immovable and unshakable rock, the moral law which the Creator Himself has manifested by means of the natural order and which He has engraved with indelible characters in the hearts of men. Within the limits of a new order founded on moral principles there is no room for the violation of the freedom, integrity and security of other states, no matter what may be their territorial extension or their capacity for defense. There is no place for open or occult oppression of the cultural or linguistic characteristics of national minorities, for the hindrance or restriction of their economic resources, for the limitation or abolition of their natural fertility." This equality of the rights of all peoples, of whatever descent, size, or power — an equality based upon the equality of all men and the oneness of mankind — involves the total rejection of the foundations of National Socialism and of Japanese missionary racialism. In his address to the German Reichstag on January 30, 1937, Adolf Hitler himself claimed the uncompromising novelty of National Socialist principles: "Fundamentally our National Socialist program puts in the place of the liberalistic concept of the individual and of the Marxist concept of mankind the folk as conditioned by blood and tied to the soil. A very simple and lapidary sentence, yet of tremendous consequences. Perhaps for the first time, since human history has begun, the understanding in this country has been directed to the goal, that of all the tasks set to us the most august and thereby the holiest for man is the preservation of the blood-bound racial kind given by God." [50] Chancellor Hitler was right: for the first time in human history the tribe has been proclaimed as the object and center of man's holiest duties. Blood and soil replace the concept of the individual (which is not only a liberalistic concept, but one common to all civilization) and that of mankind (which again is not a Marxist concept but one common to all civilization). If National Socialism had only rejected "liberalistic" (whatever that may mean) and Marxian concepts, it could not claim that it has created an understanding without precedent, a new foundation for the first time since human history began.

National Socialism has never hesitated to identify Roman Catholicism, Protestant liberalism, and Russian communism as one and the same enemy. The official "thinker" of the

National Socialist movement, Alfred Rosenberg, the intellectual mentor of Adolf Hitler and editor of the two leading party organs, the *Völkischer Beobachter* and the *Nationalsozialistische Monatshefte*, has quoted with enthusiastic approval a sentence by Paul de Lagarde, whom he exalts as the first and greatest mind who has clearly expressed the German eternal dream. "Catholicism, Protestantism, Judaism, naturalism," Lagarde wrote, "must give way completely before a new world outlook, so that they will not even be remembered any more, as the night lamp is not remembered any more, when the morning sun has risen above the mountains — or Germany's unity will become more questionable from day to day." [51] Catholicism, Protestantism, Judaism, rational liberalism, and communism — they all emphasize the oneness of mankind, they all oppose tribalism. National Socialism can compromise with Japanese tribalism, in spite of its emphasis on the Aryan or Nordic race; [52] it can never compromise with any universal doctrine. Free Masonry, Roman Catholicism,

Marxism, may oppose each other in bitter hostility; to National Socialism they are fundamentally one and the same enemy. National Socialism pits the "constructive thought" of Nordic blood "against the ideas of Free Masonry, Judaism, Marxism and the Roman Church, which are hostile to life and destructive of nations." [53] In his relentless and radical fight against Christianity, Rosenberg called the climaxing chapter of his *Myth of the Twentieth Century* "The End of Boniface" — the end of an epoch started by Wynfrith, the Anglo-Saxon, who, with a band of missionary helpers from his native England, became the apostle to the Germans and organized their Church in the first half of the eighth century. He founded the See of Mainz and the Abbey of Fulda, the oldest centers of Christian radiation in Germany, and died as a martyr, massacred by Frisian heathens. Now, twelve hundred years later, Rosenberg proclaims triumphantly the end of Boniface's work, its defeat by that blood which once created Odin and Baldur. The death of "the myth of the cross" is hailed, while "Odin lives today as he did five thousand years ago as the eternal mirror of the psychic forces of Nordic men." [54] Christianity, with its stress upon the brotherhood of man, its catholic character, its gospel of charity and love, has undermined the Nordic soul. "Today it is clear to every sincere German that this doctrine of love which embraces equally all creatures in this world has dealt a telling blow to the soul of Nordic Europe." [55]

There is little certainty about the soul of Nordic Europe. It may even not exist. Was not Rembrandt, the first who broke with the conventional misrepresentation of the Jewish type in Christian art and discovered and presented the human nobility in the features of the inhabitants of the Ghetto, as good an embodiment of the creative forces of the soul of Nordic Europe as Rosenberg? But whatever the "doctrine of love which embraces equally all men" may have done to the soul of Nordic Europe, one thing is certain: that an unbridgeable gulf separates, above all in the opinion of the National Socialists themselves, their principles from

Christianity. Not only from Christianity in all its forms; the abyss between National Socialism and all other forces of civilization, Islam and Buddhism, rational liberalism and Marxism, is equally great.[56] There exist certain affinities between National Socialism and the different forms of civilization: secularism links National Socialism and rational liberalism; authoritarianism, National Socialism and the Roman Catholic Church; total mobilization, National Socialism and Marxian communism — yet all these similarities never reach to the fundamentals. The oneness of mankind and the common destiny of all history, first proclaimed by the Hebrew prophets, have become the common inheritance of Christianity, of rational liberalism, and of Marxism. Not accidentally has National Socialism regarded the Jews as the anti-Race which must be annihilated by the Race.[57] Yet the faith in the oneness of mankind is not reserved to the West, all nationalism and racial separatism have been even more alien to Islam, Buddhism, and other Eastern religions than to Christianity. Japan in its revolt against Chinese civilization and Buddhism repeats the German revolt against Western civilization. For the crisis is not only a struggle — the struggle meant by Mein Kampf — between tribalism and Christianity, it is a life-and-death combat for the meaning of life of every man, in which the coöperation of all great religions of the East and of the West is necessary. This titanic and fantastic war against all civilization, this turn to pre-history and to the forces of myth and blood and soil, to Odin and Amaterasu, challenges all mankind, East and West alike. And in this challenge lies the incalculable danger of total catastrophe, but also the great promise and hope.

8

For this unprecedented world-wide attack on the oneness of mankind, this deification of ancient tribalism and its mythical traditions, comes at the very moment when for the first time mankind is becoming one, not in prophecy and vision, but in the reality of intercourse and exchange, and when the rational ordering of law has become imperative as never before. Marx had foreseen this development at a time when barely its first traces had become visible, when the Far East and Africa were still unknown continents, and when the steam engine had only started to revolutionize modes of communication. In 1848 he wrote: "By the exploitation of the world market, the bourgeoisie has given the cosmopolitan character to production and consumption in every land. To the despair of the reactionaries, it has deprived industry of its national foundation. The old local and national self-sufficiency and isolation are replaced by a system of universal intercourse, of all-round inter-dependence of the nations. We see this in intellectual production no less than in material. National exclusiveness and particularism are fast becoming impossible." Now, one hundred years later, this process has come to its end; modern technique and industrialism have laid the material foundations for the unity of mankind; democracy based upon the rights of man has carried its universal message destined for all peoples to the four corners of the earth; economically, spiritually, and politically all problems demand world-wide and rational solutions. An unprecedented challenge has been thrown down to man; its manifestation is the world-wide crisis. At such a critical turning point of history, nationalism, as it has developed in the last one hundred and fifty years, becomes the major obstacle to any hopeful response to the challenge; every appeal to historical rights undermines the hopes of the living for the future. German romanticism claimed nationalism as an eternal and natural force, as an indestructible part of *Gottes natürlicher Schöpfungsordnung*, of God's created natural order. All historical evidence proves the falsity of this favorite thesis of nationalism. The present German and Japanese tribalism may turn out to be the last and especially violent form of a general disease which has lately undermined the spiritual, political, and economic well-being of mankind. If this abscess is cured, before it succeeds in poisoning the whole body, the Great Society [58] which has come into being during the last one hundred years simultaneously with the spread of nationalism may find the ways and means for the rational and world-wide solution of its spiritual, political, and economic needs.

During the nineteenth century all peoples, even in the most distant lands, awakened to nationalism. They began to stress and to overstress their selfhood; they strove for independence in all fields of human activity; their masses were roused to political activity through patriotism. This process proved a great blessing to the peoples; it awakened them from their age-old lethargy, and drew them into the dynamism of modern life. Yet it is the very spread of nationalism and industrialism over all the earth which has made the continuation of the national framework of cultural, political, and economic organization incongruous with the new reality of interdependence. Political nationalism, based upon historical rights and territorial roots, has become today as obsolete as political religion, rooted historically and territorially, became by the end of the seventeenth century.[59] It was the very violence of religious claims and wars in the seventeenth century that produced the rational Enlightenment of the eighteenth century which de-politized religion. Out of the violent claims and wars of nationalism in our time a similar age of Enlightenment and of a de-politization of nationalism may ensue. The response to the present crisis cannot be found on national nor even on continental or hemispheric lines. The war, as it spreads, destroys not only the myths of national, but also of continental and hemispheric independence.

National Socialism has realized it from the beginning. Therein reposed its strength. The weakness of its adversaries in all continents rested upon their misunderstanding of the present crisis, made possible by the fact that their attention was centered upon Europe, upon the Peace Treaty of Versailles, upon Germany and her claims. But with the outbreak of the Second World War in 1936 it became clear that "this is not merely a European problem. It seems obsolete to think today of an isolated Europe. The regional and continental framework will quickly become as obsolete as the national. With all due regard to geographic and historic differences, it can safely be stated that China is fighting today the same battle as Spain." So it appeared in 1937 — and since then it has become more and more manifest that to respond to the world-wide challenge Europeans and Americans must disenthrall themselves from the traditional Europe-centered view. A European federation, though desirable as every federation of equals is, would present in itself no solution. Europe is neither politically nor economically a unit. Its boundaries are not fixed. A "unification" of Europe alone might be no progress in assuring peace and order; it might become a starting point for inter-continental wars, a basis for a struggle for the control of the globe against other continental units, against other *Grossräume*. It is understandable as a favorite theme of National Socialism. With many liberals it is a cherished remnant of the best and noblest hopes of nineteenth century thought. But it is no longer enough. In itself no good purpose is served by doing away with small states, as is sometimes claimed by the proponents of a "unified" Europe. Small nations do not represent a greater danger to peace and prosperity than great nations do. Denmark and the Netherlands, Switzerland and Norway, led culturally as intense and economically as progressive an existence as any great and powerful state. Their citizens were happy and contented; in spite of their small territory they did not suffer from a claustrophobia which would have urged them on towards the conquest of greater living space. Economically they were not more unsound than large states; these, and even whole continents, may become by high tariff walls as great a menace to world trade as small states. The economic world crisis of the 'thirties did not originate in Nicaragua or Yugoslavia, but in the United States. Bigness in itself is neither politically nor economically a remedy; and the spirit never depended upon space. True, small nations cannot stand alone in the present world and defend their existence. But experience has shown that under present conditions very great nations cannot stand alone either. Neither bigness of territory nor great distances have saved Canada or Australia from the danger of invasion, though the realization of the danger came to them as a sudden shock. The British Empire, the United States of America, the Soviet Union, China, nations which represent in varying degrees vast agglomerations of man-power, of territory, of resources, some of them rather continents or sub-continents than nations, have begun to understand that even they cannot stand alone under the conditions of modern warfare and that they would be helpless if standing alone. Their illusion of possible neutrality or self-sufficiency as a result of their bigness was more dangerous than the similar illusion of Norway or Switzerland. It may even be asked whether for the growth of democracy the small state does not represent the more propitious basis of organization, and whether it might not be desirable, in the interests of peace and of human progress, to divide up large and centralized states into smaller ones.

The federation of several states in any part of the earth may eliminate wars and frictions among them; it would not promote peace nor economic prosperity nor democratic freedom. These can be established today only on a world-wide basis of equalitarian law and rational intercourse, law enforced by superior force and intercourse freed from traditional shackles. The present crisis is not the result of the disorder of one continent — Europe — nor the affair of one race — the white race. It is the immense and incalculable implication of this crisis, it is its unique promise, that Europe and the white race do not occupy any longer the central position of former centuries. The prologue to the tragedy of the 'thirties was enacted in Manchuria, not on the Rhine. It has been rightly said that the American frontier is on the Rhine; it still is there, but it is also on the Mekong and on the Dnieper, and it may be tomorrow on the Niger. This is a world crisis, the first total and global crisis, deciding in a total way the fate of the globe. This war is neither in its origin nor in its consequences a European

war, it is a world war. But it is not a world
war between continents or races. It is not
"Europe's" or "Asia's" war against "alien" or
raumfremd interference, a war between continents and their "Monroe doctrines." Nor is
it, what some American fascists would have
welcomed, a war of the white or Nordic race
against inferior races, against Asiatic Russia
or the Yellow Peril. This is as little a racial
war as it is a European or an Asiatic war. It
is a war in which on both sides all races are
involved, a war the outcome of which will
determine the future of all races on earth.
Germany and Japan are fighting on one side,
not only because their strategic interests coincide, but because their image of man and
their understanding of history are similar.
Their opponents can win the war, overcome
the crisis, and establish peace only if they
disenthrall themselves from their parochial
and sectional views, from their racial preoc-
cupations, from not only national isolationism but continental provincialism — for continents represent in the twentieth century
what provinces did in the eighteenth and na-

tions in the nineteenth. As the religions of
East and West must learn to coöperate, as
the ecumenical movement will reach beyond
Christianity, so the Second World War can
be won for mankind only by the closest co-
operation of men of all races and every color.
The survival of the United States and of
Great Britain is interdependent with that of
the Soviet Union and of China. By a strange
irony of history the devastating blows suf-
fered by the United States and Great Britain
in the Pacific at the hands of Japan have established a new basis for racial coöperation
and equality. As Japan's victory over Russia
in 1905 became the signal for the awakening
of the colored races in Asia and Africa, the
starting point of their new and startling activities for equality and emancipation,[60] so
did the disaster at Pearl Harbor and the fall
of Hong Kong, Manila, and Singapore, of
the proud bastions of white prestige, of the
outposts of the seemingly most powerful empires, herald throughout the cities and forests, the mountains and deserts, of Asia and
Africa the spectacular end of an epoch, ap-

parently so firmly established at the end of
the nineteenth century. The news of it
has spread immediately and unmistakably
through village, tent and kraal. With a stroke
a world crumbled; a new one can arise.

It will not be the tribal world of Japan's
and Germany's empires, if the free people
will, at this late hour, rise to a full understanding of the crisis. Japan has announced
her conquests as the liberation of Asia. But
the Asiatic peoples remember the martyrdom of the Koreans as the European peoples,
against similar "liberating" claims of Germany, remember the Calvary of Poland. At
this late hour entirely new perspectives of
possible conduct and action open before mankind. They emerge on all continents. They
are not confined to any race. For the first
time in history a ruler of China has left the
Middle Kingdom and gone to India; in the
land which has been the heart of the British
Empire, in an unprecedented and momentous
interview with India's leaders the yellow and
the brown men have broken new ground for
the reordering of the world. At Africa's stra-

tegic crossroads from the Atlantic to the Indian Ocean, in the great French colonial province of Chad where about five hundred white men live among one and a half million Negroes, the governor-general, Eboué, has probably done more to keep Africa safe for the democratic cause and to facilitate the communication from West Africa to the Middle East than any other single man. "Eboué is a black man of heavy build and great majesty, much blacker than any of his subjects in Equatorial Africa. He was born in the West Indies, acquired his status as a French citizen, passed all his examinations like any Frenchman, and ran up the gamut of the colonial administration. He was governing the Chad when France crashed. He was the first governor to join de Gaulle, and he gave the white race an example of integrity, courage and decision that will go down the centuries to the honour of the black races, and to the honour of that France that gave them their chance." [61] The United States and Great Britain may yet be saved, in their life-and-death struggle against the white and yellow men of Germany and Japan, by the yellow men of China and the black men of Africa, the Indians and the Negroes, the Arabs and the Malays. They will be saved by disenthralling themselves from the narrowness of their vision, by a new world view and a true catholicity which will live up to the universal message of all civilization, of Christianity and of democracy. It is the unique and distinguishing character of this greatest crisis in human history that the survival and the victory of all free peoples depends upon their becoming and remaining United Nations. The immense and incalculable danger of the present crisis can only be overcome in a way which justifies an immense and incalculable hope.

9

The crisis forces mankind to seek new ways. In times like these daring is needed and becomes possible. Germany and Japan owe their success in the crisis to daring. They have been from the beginning aware of the unprecedented crisis-character of the time:

they have realized the immense stakes involved and have taken the initiative which has stunned the free peoples who have continued to think in the accepted and conventional ways. Germany and Japan have shown an unexpected strength because they regarded nothing as improbable or even impossible today, while the free peoples remained within the possibilities and probabilities of yesterday. New situations demand new creative responses. Under stress of necessity men are capable of decisions and realizations which they never would have envisaged otherwise. The free peoples of the earth are today in a situation in which there is no survival for them except as United Nations. The crisis-situation is a result of historical development, of the dynamism of the forces of democracy, industrial technology, and nationalism, which in mutual support and conflict have shaped the background out of which the crisis grew. But in their historical texture the possible solution of the crisis is delineated. Democracy, technology, nationalism, all point toward harmonization in the United Nations.

The difficulties in the way of the realization of this new situation are tremendous. It has always been easier for men to sacrifice their lives and even their fortunes than to abandon their habitual ways of thought and feeling, their prejudices and traditions. To think and feel nationally has been ingrained in men's minds in the age of nationalism; it demands great wisdom and courage to see that in the present crisis nationalism is not enough. All nations harbour feelings of jealousies and distrust against other nations. The peace of 1919 was wrecked not by "hatred against Germany" or "desire of vengeance," which both, so far as they existed by 1919, evaporated fast in Great Britain and in the United States, but by the mutual jealousies and distrust which immediately after November 11, 1918, animated the peoples of the Allied and Associated nations, the peoples and not only their leaders. The words which Norman Angell wrote in 1917, in his book *The Political Conditions of Allied Success*, cannot be repeated often enough. They pointed the right way then. They were not heeded, though they were truly prophetic, inspired by a rational vision of reality. They point the right way now:

"The survival of the Western democracies, in so far as that is a matter of the effective use of their force, depends upon their capacity to use it as a unit, during the War and after. That unity we have not attained, even for the purposes of the War, because we have refused to recognize its necessary conditions — a kind and degree of democratic internationalism to which current political ideas and feelings are hostile; an internationalism which is not necessary to the enemy, but is to us. He can in some measure ignore it. We cannot. His unity, in so far as it rests upon moral factors, can be based upon the old nationalist conceptions; our unity depends upon a revision of them, an enlargement into an internationalism. The greatest obstacles to a permanent association of nations by which the security of each shall be made to rest upon the strength of the whole are disbelief in its feasibility and our subjection to the traditions of national sovereignty and independence. Were it generally believed in, and desired, it would be not only feasible but inevitable. Return to the old relationships after the War will sooner or later doom the democratic nations, however powerful each may be individually, to subjugation in detail by a group, inferior in power but superior in material unity — a unity which autocracy achieves at the cost of freedom and human worth."

Woodrow Wilson had the same vision: there could be no peace without world order. Now, after the coming of the Second World War, foreseen by Angell and Wilson, the problem is still the same but its challenge is infinitely greater — the threat of total ruin involved is immeasurably more menacing, the need of recovery urgent as never before. Not only will there be no lasting peace without world order, there will be no survival for the United States or the Soviet Union, for Great Britain or China, no victory for the free peoples, without the closest coöperation of the United Nations. The mutual jealousies and reproaches, distrusts, and fears, so potent and understandable in the light of the very recent past, are the most powerful allies that Germany and Japan can find. They help and accelerate the solution of the crisis in the sense in which the fascist powers wish to solve it. This solution would lead to the ruin of civilization. It can recover only through the realization of its basis, which fascism rejects and destroys, the universality of rational law and the interdependence of mankind.

Though men may not seem ready for it, the time is. And hopeful signs point through the fury of the widening war towards a greater understanding and a greater readiness of the minds than anybody could expect at the beginning of the fateful and crucial year of 1940. Great Britain's offer of a union with France in June 1940 was the sign at the turn of the times. The declaration of friendship signed in Moscow on December 4, 1941, between the government of the Soviet Union and the government of the Polish Republic is another. For many centuries Russians and Poles have been bitter enemies. Distrust, fears, and hatreds had accumulated and had been sharply accentuated during the last twenty years when an abyss of hostility separated Soviet Communism and deeply conservative, semi-fascist, Roman Catholic Poland. It was not merely a theoretical or ideological hostility, for the two countries had long frontiers in common, without any natural barrier, burdened with the memory of the only war which the two countries had fought from 1919 to 1939, a war fought against each other. Yet the improbable happened: they have now laid the foundations for exemplary coöperation in war and peace.[62] Necessity forced this complete change; it points to many other hopeful and surprising signs in the same direction. The Czechoslovakia of Masaryk and the Poland of Pilsudski had little in common; now the two countries have concluded a pact outlining their future close federation after the war. Under men like General Sikorski and Professor Kot, a Poland fundamentally different from that of Colonel Beck is emerging. Though life in the Soviet Union is conditioned by Marx's absolutization of the class war and his relativization of truth and ethics, and by the historical traditions of the Russian masses unaccustomed to individualism and democracy as forms of life, its government has followed throughout a foreign policy based upon peace and an internal policy based upon the complete equality of all races, European and Asiatic, and the equalization of the standards of life of all peoples, progressive and backward. The peace of 1919 was vitiated by the absence of Russia from the peace table; the peace after the Second World War can be assured by the inclusion of the Soviet Union as a United Nation.

Though words are in themselves not creating realities and though they are often abused to cover hypocrisies and falsehood, irresolution and half-heartedness, nevertheless they have an indicative force. During the First World War, when the immense threat to the survival of free nations was not yet clearly recognized, there were Allied and Associated nations. This time, in the lateness of the hour, there are United Nations. This change of name, spontaneously and quickly accepted, is indicative of the changing attitude. A similar progress can be seen in many other directions. The relations between the United States and the Latin American republics have fundamentally changed, if compared with 1916 when an American Expeditionary Force under General Pershing marched into Mexico, and when American marines were in control of the Dominican Republic, Haiti, and Nicaragua. The Lend-Lease arrangements as defined in the Act of Congress of March 11, 1941, bear witness again to a similar immense and readily accepted progress over the war debt arrangements of the First World War, a progress which a very short while before would have seemed unbelievable. The preamble of the Agreement sets forth this new situation in declaring that the United States and Great Britain "are engaged in a coöperative undertaking, together with every other nation or people with like mind, to the end of laying the bases of a just and enduring world peace securing order under law to themselves and all nations." Though the difficulties ahead are still tremendous and the vested emotional interests of the thought-processes of yesterday still widely entertained, the United Nations begin to emerge more rapidly than could be expected as the foundation of world order. In 1910 an American citizen, Mr. Hamilton Holt, wrote: "The United States furnishes the model for the united nations. The Declaration of Independence foreshadows the declaration of interdependence." [63] Thirty years later, in March 1941, the House of Representatives and the Senate of the State of North Carolina adopted a joint resolution for a Declaration of the Federation of the World,[64] in which it was said: "The corner stone of totalitarianism is the ethnographic State, whose restricted interests define the scope of its favors; the foundation of democracy is man whose integrity is inviolable and whose welfare is its primary concern. . . . Man has struggled from time immemorial to endow the individual with certain fundamental rights whose very existence is now imperiled. . . . Man must now either consolidate his historic rights or lose them for generations to come. . . . Just as feudalism served its purpose in human history and was superseded by nationalism, so has nationalism reached its apogee in this generation and yielded its hegemony in the body politic to internationalism. . . . It is better for the world to be ruled by an international sovereignty of reason, social justice and peace than by diverse national sovereignties organically incapable of preventing their own dissolution by conquest. Mankind must pool its resources of defense if civilization is to endure. . . . Federation vitalizes all nations by endowing them with security and freedom to develop their respective cultures without menace of foreign domination. It regards as sacrosanct man's personality, his rights as an individual and as a citizen and his role as a partner with all other men in the common enterprise of building civilization for the benefit of mankind. It suppresses the crime of war by reducing to the ultimate minimum the possibility of its occurrence. It renders unnecessary the further paralyzing expenditure of wealth for belligerent activity. . . . It apprehends the entire human race as one family, human beings everywhere as brothers and all nations as component parts of an indivisible community. There is no alternative to the federation of all nations except endless war."

There is no time yet for premature blue prints. The things to come will be shaped by the unfolding events of the war. It is the intention that counts, the intention that will shape the war and the ensuing peace; not an intention of vague hopes, but of a clear will. The needs for survival force men into new ways. Only United Nations, developing a growing sense of unity, can win the war. If they remain united they can establish a world order, based upon the rule of law among nations and bills of rights and duties within nations. Without the rule of law there can be no disarmament nor peace. No nation can disarm in a lawless world. But law is only law if it is enforced; peace is durable only when backed by the necessary force. Wars in self-defense or for self-interest are the sign of a society still primitive internationally. Force used for the enforcement of law is necessary to the protection of civilized society against the inroads of barbarism. Even within a peaceful world no panaceas for social and economic ills will be found. There are no short cuts to perfection, only the painful and gradual but relentless and tenacious march forward to greater plenty more equally shared by all. This task is there at all times, not only in this crisis. The promise held out in this crisis is not economic benefits, but a lawful order within which the freedom and dignity of man can develop. Yet the world-wide order will facilitate and make possible the solution of the economic and social problems of modern interdependent industrial and agrarian society. It will result in a higher standard of life in the "backward" or under-privileged countries, it will open up tremendous opportunities for public works and engineering, for health and education in the vast underdeveloped parts of the world; with the creation of a world-wide framework for economic exchange and coöperation, and

with peace and security assured, the energies
of man can be directed into the most productive channels. The civilized society of the
future will be a society of growing bounty.

Civilized society is at stake in the present
crisis. Its survival depends upon the emergence of world order out of the world crisis.
This can happen only through a revival of
the fundamental attitudes of democracy, a
reconsideration of nationalism, a resumption
of the old imperial idea based upon the oneness of mankind and of civilization. The
three changing concepts of democracy, nationalism, and imperialism, reflect three aspects of the crisis; the response, expressed
in their transformation, is rooted in the historical development of the centuries and in
the actual necessity of the hour. The challenge of fascism has made the crisis manifest;
it has made the nation absolute and sacri-
ficed to it the individual and mankind, the
two fundamental concepts of civilization.
The victory of fascism will ruin civilization,
which can recover only by working out the
implications of democracy and of religion

through realizing the universal promise of empire — peace and justice; a realization for which for the first time the necessary conditions exist. Every tendency towards separation, segregation, and exclusiveness, whether based on historical "rights" or biological "laws" of nature, undermines the hopes for the defeat of the fascist challenge and for a peaceful order at the very time when the growth of interdependence and mutuality is ready to mature the seed of the future. There out of the crisis civilization can recover: in a new democracy of man, conscious of his limitations and of the reality of evil, who is dignified as the subject of moral law and as a partner of humanity; in a new nationalism, de-demonized and de-politized, resting upon free association and liberated from the dead weight of the past; and in a new imperialism, which will take up again, under the changed conditions of modern technology and with the experience of the ages, their ancient and ever-new promise of a world order based upon a community of law.

NOTES

NOTES

CHAPTER ONE

1. Don M. Wolfe, *Milton in the Puritan Revolution* (New York, 1941), p. 36.

2. John Wise, *A Vindication of the Government of New England Churches* (Boston, 1860), p. 40.

3. *The Works of John Adams*, 10 vols. (Boston, 1856), I, 66.

4. *The Works of Benjamin Franklin*, 10 vols. (Boston, 1840), II, 469.

5. *Letters from an American Farmer*, by J. Hector St. John (Philadelphia, 1793), p. 46 f.

6. *The Writings of Thomas Jefferson*, 9 vols. (Washington, 1853–54), IV, 318; VII, 27.

7. *The Writings of Thomas Jefferson*, 20 vols. (Washington, 1903), X, 325.

8. Noah Webster, *Sketches of American Policy*, ed. by Harry R. Warfel (New York, 1937), p. 23.

9. *The Political Writings of Joel Barlow* (New York, 1796), p. 142.

10. *The Writings of Thomas Jefferson*, 10 vols. (New York, 1892–99), VIII, 8.

11. *The Writings of Thomas Jefferson*, 9 vols. (Washington, 1853–54), VII, 450.

12. Albert K. Weinberg, *Manifest Destiny* (Baltimore, 1935), p. 124.

13. *The Federalist*, ed. by Henry Cabot Lodge (New York, 1908), p. 81.

14. *The Writings of George Washington* (New York, 1891), XI, 58 f.

15. See René Avord, "Le Romantisme de la Violence," *La France Libre*, vol. I (1941), No. 6.

16. Arnold Oskar Meyer, "Aus der Geschichte des deutschen Nationalgefühls," *Deutsche und Engländer: Wesen und Werden in grosser Geschichte* (Munich, 1937), p. 42.

17. *Sämtliche Werke* (Leipzig, 1794–1801), XV, 362. See the whole passage beginning on page 359.

18. See *Force or Reason* (3rd ed., Cambridge, Mass., 1938), and "The Totalitarian Philosophy of War," in *Not by Arms Alone* (Cambridge, Mass., 1940).

19. Paul Joachimsen, "Zur historischen Psychologie des deutschen Staatsgedankens," *Die Dioskuren*, I (Munich, 1922), 157.

20. Paul Joachimsen, *op. cit.*, p. 152. "Die Erlösung der sittlichen Bedürftigkeit im Staate und durch den Staat ist das Kennzeichen des deutschen Staatsgedankens geblieben," *ibid.*, p. 170.

21. Paul Joachimsen, *op. cit.*, p. 116.

22. See *Revolutions and Dictatorships* (2nd. ed.), Cambridge, Mass., 1941, chapter vii.

23. See Thomas Mann "Denken und Leben," *The Virginia Quarterly Review*, Summer 1941; Crane Brinton, *Nietzsche* (Cambridge, Mass., 1941); J. A. Cramb, *Germany and England* (New York, 1914), pp. 126–130.

24. *The Complete Works*, ed. by Dr. Oscar Levy, XVI, 94.

25. *Ibid.*, XIII, 40.

26. *Hour of Decision* (New York, 1934), p. 19.

27. *The Uncollected Poetry and Prose of Walt Whitman*, ed. by Emory Holloway (Garden City, N. Y., 1921), I, 159. There also: "Is not this better than the despairing apathy wherewith the populace of Russia and . . . the miserable German states — those *well-ordered* governments — endure the black-hearted rapacity of their rulers?"

28. See E. Y. Hartshorne, *German Youth and the Nazi Dream of Victory* (New York, 1941), and especially Gregor Ziemer, *Education for Death* (Oxford Uni-

versity Press, 1941). The German lines below may be translated as follows:

"The decaying bones of the world tremble before
    the great war.
  We have broken its terror; ours was the great vic-
    tory.
  We shall march on, when everything crumbles.
  Today Germany belongs to us, tomorrow the
    whole world."

29. Benedetto Croce in *Freedom, Its Meaning*, ed. by Ruth Nanda Anshen (New York, 1940), pp. 24 f., 41.

CHAPTER TWO

1. Aristotle understood by "state," or "fatherland," something that could easily be felt as a reality in everyday concrete contacts. He therefore believed that a state should consist of not less than ten, and of not more than ten thousand, inhabitants (*Ethics*, IX, 10, 3). The great barbarian empires were for him no real states (*Politics*, VII, 4).

2. Robert Michels has remarked that the *Fernstenliebe* extends from patriotism to internationalism. "Denn Patriotismus und Internationalismus haben das Merkmal physischer Kontaktlosigkeit der sie Empfindenden zu den Mitempfindenden gemeinsam" (*Der Patriotismus; Prolegomena zu seiner soziologischen Analyse*, Munich 1929, p. 88). Patriotism and internationalism are, or can be, the product of an historical development and of indoctrination by education.

3. W. B. Pillsbury, *The Psychology of Nationality and Internationalism* (New York, 1919), p. 5. The last chapter of this book is especially worthy of attention.

4. Israel Zangwill, *The Principle of Nationalities* (London, 1917), p. 39. Max Weber defines nationality as "a common bond of sentiment whose adequate expression would be a state of its own, and which there-

fore normally tends to give birth to such a state" (*Verhandlungen des Zweiten Deutschen Soziologentages*, Tübingen 1913, p. 50).

5. Hans Kohn, "The Genesis and Character of English Nationalism," *Journal of the History of Ideas*, I (1940), 69–94.

6. "The spirit of nationality may be defined (negatively but not inaccurately) as a spirit which makes people feel and act and think about a part of any given society as though it were the whole of that society" (Arnold J. Toynbee, *A Study of History*, London 1934, I, 9).

7. Sidney Herbert, *Nationality and Its Problems* (London, 1920), p. 161.

8. Robert E. Park and Ernest W. Burgess, *Introduction to the Science of Sociology* (Chicago, 1924), p. 931.

9. See *Revolutions and Dictatorships* (Cambridge, Mass., 1939), pp. 240–246.

CHAPTER THREE

1. When Diodorus of Sicily made Nicholas of Syracuse plead for the captive Athenians, he put into his mouth their praise as the first who had taught the Greeks the cultivation of that sweet nourishment received from the gods and afterwards becoming of common use: "Did they not invent laws which have changed the common life from a beastly and uncivilized existence into a gentle and civilized community? Have they not been the first to establish the right of asylum for exiles and given in favor of the suppliants laws which were respected by all men?" (*Bibliotheca Historica*, XIII, 26).

2. Aristotle thought Hellas could shoulder the Greek man's burden of "ruling all mankind if it attain constitutional unity" (*Politics*, VII, vi. 1–1327b).

3. *De fortuna Alexandri*, I, 6, 329b, c.

4. "Thou hast made a common fatherland for different nations;

Useful it was for the unjust, to be caught under thy domination.

While thou offerest to the vanquished the community of thine own law,

Thou hast turned into one state what had been previously the globe."

5. "Der Weg der Germanen war nicht das Erlösungsbedürfnis — das kannten sie nicht. Auch nicht die Frage nach dem Sittengesetz — das trugen sie in sich als Wille zur tapferen Selbstbehauptung und zur Wahrung der Sippenehre." (Arnold Oskar Meyer, *Deutsche und Engländer*, Munich 1937, p. 5.)

6. Orosius, *Historiae Livri VII Adversus Paganos*, VII, 43.

7. *Monumenta Germaniae Historica: Poetae Latini Aevi Carolini*, II, (Berlin, 1884), 559–564.

"Floruit egregium claro diademate regnum,
   Princeps unus erat, populus quoque subditus unus;
   Lex simul et iudex totas ornaverat urbes,
   Pax cives tenuit, virtus exterruit hostes. . . .
Quid faciant populi, quos ingens alluit Hister,
   Quos Renus Rhodanusque rigant Ligerusve Padusve;
   Quos omnes dudum tenuit concordia nexos,
   Foedere nunc rupto divortia mesta fatigant."

8. See my article, "Spanish Imperialism: A Dream Resumed," *The American Scholar*, VIII (1939), 321–332.

9. See my article, "The Genesis and Character of English Nationalism," *Journal of the History of Ideas*, I (1940), 69–94.

10. Macaulay on Milton, *Critical, Historical, and Miscellaneous Essays* (New York, 1860), I, 233. Milton identified the English people with the cause of individ-

ual liberty, freedom of conscience, and the dignity of reason. Many Englishmen thought of England in the seventeenth century as the center of a *Weltpolitik* of universal liberty.

11. Albert K. Weinberg, *Manifest Destiny. A Study of Nationalist Expansionism in American History* (Baltimore, 1935), pp. 124, 283, and *passim*.

12. "Canada gives them [the United States] so little uneasiness that their thoughts are much more turned towards annexing the country themselves, an enterprise in which I for one heartily wish them success" (Heinrich von Treitschke, *Politics*, tr. by Blanche Dugdale, London, 1916, II, 300).

13. When Emperor William II addressed the German troops embarked for China on July 3, 1900, with the well-known words: "Kommt ihr vor den Feind, so wird derselbe geschlagen! Wer euch in die Hände fällt, sei euch verfallen! Wie vor tausend Jahren die Hunnen unter ihrem König Etzel sich einen Namen gemacht, der sie noch jetzt in Überlieferung und Märchen gewaltig erscheinen lässt, so möge der Name Deutscher in China auf tausend Jahre durch euch in einer Weise betätigt werden, dass niemals wieder ein Chinese es wagt, einen Deutschen auch nur scheel anzusehen," few people even in Germany took his threats seriously. They knew that the restraining influences which prevented the return of the age of the Huns were too strong in Germany then.

14. Nicolas Zernov, *Moscow the Third Rome* (London, 1937), pp. 47, 49.

15. "Das deutsche Volk, das adeligste der Welt, von Gott auserwählt zur Würde des Imperiums, das Kaisertum von überirdischem Glanz umstrahlt, bestimmt zur Erlösung der Menschheit von Unfrieden und Sünde, darum notwendig die Verdeutschung der gesamten Welt, auch der romanischen Völker, unter der Oberhoheit des deutschen Kaisers, das sind die ausschweifenden, überschwänglichen Phantasien, die hier, an der

Schwelle der Neuzeit, sich an die Reichsidee heften"
(Richard Scholz in *Neue Jahrbücher für Deutsche Wissenschaft*, vol. XIII, 1937, no. 1, p. 39. Cf. Edward
Fueter, *Geschichte der neueren Historiographie*, 3rd
ed., Munich 1936, pp. 181 ff.).

16. "Der deutsche Imperialismus, der jüngste von
allen, ist ganz anderer Art gewesen. Er teilt mit seinen
Namensvettern nur den wirtschaftlichen Ursprung. . . .
Die besondere Schwierigkeit für den deutschen Imperialismus lag darin, dass die deutsche Wirtschaft, die
ihn tragen sollte, durchaus an den Staat gebunden, ein
staatliches Machtinstrument geworden war. Damit bedeutete Ausdehnung der Wirtschaft auch Ausdehnung
der Staatsmacht in einem ganz anderen Sinne als etwa
in England." (Paul Joachimsen, "Zur Psychologie des
deutschen Staatsgedankens," *Die Dioskuren*, I, Munich,
1922, 166, 167.) On the similar attitudes of Prussia and
Japan see *Not By Arms Alone* (Cambridge, Mass.,
1940), pp. 121 f.

17. Thorstein Veblen, *An Inquiry into the Nature of
Peace and the Terms of its Perpetuation* (New York,
1917), p. 201. Veblen warns that "no engagement
binds a dynastic statesman in case it turns out not to
further the dynastic enterprise" (p. 83) and deprecates
strongly any negotiated peace with dynastic imperialism, because such a peace would necessarily "be an
armistice terminable at will and serving as a season of
preparation to meet a deferred opportunity. For the
peaceable nations it would, in effect, be a respite and a
season of preparation for eventual submission to the
Imperial rule" (p. 87, cf. 84).

18. See the remarks by Philip Rahv in *The Partisan
Review*, VIII (1941), 503.

19. F. M. Kircheisen, *Napoleon*, tr. by Henry St.
Lawrence (New York, 1932), pp. 552, 391.

20. F. M. Kircheisen, *Napoleon's Autobiography*, tr.
by Frederick Collins (New York, 1931), p. 256.

21. *Ibid.*, p. 230.

22. See Oswald Spengler, *Der Untergang des Abendlandes*, II (Munich, 1922), 552 ff., and my *Revolutions and Dictatorships* (Cambridge, Mass., 1939), pp. 38 ff.

23. Richard W. Tims, *Germanizing Prussian Poland* (New York, 1941), p. 282.

24. "Entweder die Welt wird regiert nach den Vorstellungen unserer modernen Demokratie, . . . oder die Welt wird beherrscht nach den Gesetzen der natürlichen Kraftordnung, dann siegen die Völker des brutalen Willens und mithin eben wieder nicht die Nation der Selbstbeschränkung." "Am Ende siegt ewig nur die Sucht der Selbsterhaltung. Unter ihr schmilzt die sogenannte Humanität als Ausdruck einer Mischung von Dummheit, Feigheit und eingebildetem Besserwissen, wie Schnee in der Märzensonne. Im ewigen Kampfe ist die Menschheit gross geworden — im ewigen Frieden geht sie zugrunde." (*Mein Kampf*, p. 148 f.) Cf. also: "Die Natur . . . setzt die Lebewesen zunächst auf diesen Erdball und sieht dem freien Spiel der Kräfte zu. Der Stärkste an Mut und Fleiss erhält dann als ihr liebstes Kind das Herrenrecht des Daseins zugesprochen" (p. 147), and "Sie glaubt somit keineswegs an eine Gleichheit der Rassen, sondern erkennt mit ihrer Verschiedenheit auch ihren höheren oder minderen Wert und fühlt sich durch diese Erkenntnis verpflichtet, gemäss dem ewigen Wollen, das dieses Universum beherrscht, den Sieg des Besseren, Stärkeren zu fördern, die Unterordnung des Schlechteren und Schwächeren zu verlangen" (p. 421). The unquestioned equation of stronger and better is characteristic.

25. Gregor Ziemer, *Education for Death* (New York, 1941), gives probably the best and most recent firsthand account of National Socialist education and aims.

26. In an address to the annual meeting of the German Academy of Law, Munich, November 22, 1940.

27. "Die Anwendung von Gewalt allein, ohne die Triebkraft einer geistigen Grundvorstellung als Voraussetzung, kann niemals zur Vernichtung einer Idee und deren Verbreitung führen, ausser in Form einer restlosen Ausrottung aber auch des letzten Trägers und der Zerstörung der letzten Überlieferung" (*Mein Kampf*, p. 187). The possibility of this sustained ruthless brutality is offered by an underlying mental attitude which aspires to become, or to impose itself as, a universal mental atittude. "In der ewig gleichmässigen Anwendung der Gewalt allein liegt die allererste Voraussetzung zum Erfolge. Diese Beharrlichkeit jedoch ist immer nur das Ergebnis einer bestimmten geistigen Überzeugung" (p. 188). "Die Überzeugung vom Recht der Anwendung selbst brutalster Waffen ist stets gebunden an das Vorhandensein eines fanatischen Glaubens an die Notwendigkeit des Sieges einer umwälzenden neuen Ordnung dieser Erde. Eine Bewegung, die nicht für solche höchste Ziele und Ideale ficht, wird daher nie zur letzten Waffe greifen" (p. 597).

28. "Einen Nationalismus als Aufstieg bestimmter innerer Werte haben wir deshalb nur bei jenen Völkern zu fördern und zu begrüssen, von denen wir glauben, dass die Kräfte ihrer Schicksalslinien mit den Ausstrahlungen des deutschen Volkes nicht in feindlichen Gegensatz geraten. . . . Wir können feststellen, dass z.B. die südafrikanischen Mischlinge oder die Mischlinge in Ostindien auch 'nationalistische' Revolutionen machen, dass die Neger von Haiti und San Domingo ein 'nationalistisches' Erwachen verspüren, dass unter der Losung vom Selbstbestimmungsrecht der Völker ganz schematisch auch alle minderwertigen Elemente auf diesem Erdball für sich Freiheit beanspruchen. Das alles interessiert uns entweder nicht oder nur insoweit, als eine weitblickende deutsche Politik die Stärkung des Germanentums sich durch ihre Verwendung verspricht und innerhalb dieses germanischen Erwachens eine Stärkung

des deutschen Volkes." (Alfred Rosenberg, *Der Mythus des 20. Jahrhunderts*, Munich, 1934, p. 644 f.)

29. Culture originated for Hitler with the enslavement of inferior races which preceded the domestication and enslavement of animals (*Mein Kampf*, p. 323). On p. 479 he calls Negroes "geborene Halbaffen" and vehemently combats their admission to and education for the liberal professions, "das Hinaufdressieren zu geistigen Berufen. Denn um eine Dressur handelt es sich dabei, genau so wie bei der des Pudels." In the unabridged translation (New York, 1940), he speaks on pages 954 ff. about the oriental, especially Indian, "fight for freedom."

30. *Mein Kampf*, pp. 173 ff. See also my *Revolutions and Dictatorships* (Cambridge, Mass., 1939), p. 343, and *Not by Arms Alone* (Cambridge, Mass., 1940), pp. 1–30.

31. "Wer z.B. den Sieg des pazifistischen Gedankens in dieser Welt wirklich von Herzen wünschen wollte, müsste sich mit allen Mitteln für die Eroberung der Welt durch die Deutschen einsetzen, . . . Tatsächlich ist die pazifistischhumane Idee vielleicht ganz gut dann, wenn der höchststehende Mensch sich vorher die Welt in einem Umfange erobert und unterworfen hat, der ihn zum alleinigen Herrn dieser Erde macht." (*Mein Kampf*, p. 315.) For other passages about the world domination by the master-race see pp. 422, 437 f., 439, 475 f., 493, 782. Pidder Lüng in his *Nationalsozialismus* well summed up the essence of the present German conception of a world order: "Every effort made towards cementing international ties, or bringing about international understanding and unification always takes its rise in individuals whose feelings are degenerate and rootless in a folkish sense, regardless of whether their motives are idealistic or economic. There is no international solidarity among plants, and there is none among animals. There is also none among men who

found their notions on the laws of nature. The idea of 'humanity' is an abstraction which cannot be translated into practical life." (*Mein Kampf*, unabridged translation, New York 1940, p. 969.)

32. The Poetic Edda, Voluspo, stanzas 44, 45.

33. See *Force or Reason* (Cambridge, Mass., 1937), pp. 77–111, 142–147.

CHAPTER FOUR

1. Arnold J. Toynbee, *Survey of International Affairs 1935* (London: Oxford University Press, 1936), II, 239 f.

2. Japan by her action of 1931 had also violated the League of Nations Covenant and the Kellogg Pact, and in addition the treaties of the Washington Conference. But still her action remained an isolated fact which did not bear fruit in an immediate and unbroken chain of further aggression and treaty violations as did the events of 1935 and 1936.

3. Toynbee, *op. cit.* pp. 355 ff.

4. On the debate about the realism of the policy of collective security see Toynbee, *op. cit.* pp. 442–482 and Sir Norman Angell, "The New John Bull," *Political Quarterly*, vol. VII (1936), no. 3.

5. "Those who wished to dam the flood of aggression when it was distant and still feeble were war-mongers; but those who were intensifying the disorder of the world by the pursuit of an isolationist foreign policy and an autarchic economic one adorned their own brows with the laurels of peace and prosperity." "The vital fact was not the strength of the forces of aggression, but the criminal weakness and futile disunion of those whose interests and ideals should have united to compel them to pursue a policy which would have maintained, at least for our time, the peace of the world."

(Alfred Cobban, *The Crisis of Civilization*, London: Cape, 1941, pp. 34, 37.)

6. A. Morgan Young, *Imperial Japan 1926–1938* (New York: Morrow, 1938), p. 283.

7. According to the *New York Herald Tribune* of February 5, 1942, the Berlin radio announced the preceding day in a broadcast for listeners in East Asia that German and Japanese gods were symbols of the "same pure Aryanism" and that Wotan was similar in character and meaning to the Japanese God of the Sun and the Winds, apparently the Sun Goddess Amaterasu, the divine ancestor of the Japanese imperial family. The broadcaster declared that "both gods are watching over their people to keep them in military and patriotic spirit."

8. Arnold J. Toynbee, *Survey of International Affairs 1937* (London: Oxford University Press, 1938), I, 327.

9. Editor, *The Nineteenth Century and After*, January 1942, p. 2.

10. Thorstein Veblen, *An Inquiry into the Nature of Peace and Terms of its Perpetuation* (New York: Macmillan, 1917), pp. 82–85. See also pp. 187, 235, 238.

11. *Ibidem*, p. 93 f. On p. 86, in a note, Veblen quotes from Eduard Meyer, *England, Its Political Organization and Development and the War against Germany*, tr. by H. S. White (Boston, 1916), p. 30 f.: "To us the state is the most indispensable as well as the highest requisite to our earthly existence. . . . All individualistic endeavor . . . must be unreservedly subordinated to this lofty claim. . . . The state . . . eventually is of infinitely more value than the sum of all the individuals within its jurisdiction." "This conception of the state, which is as much a part of our life as is the blood in our veins, is nowhere to be found in the English Constitution, and is quite foreign to English thought, and to that of America as well."

12. Of Veblen's *Imperial Germany and the Industrial*

Revolution Dr. Joseph Dorfman said in his introduction
to the new edition (New York: Viking, 1939): "So well
had Veblen caught the spirit of the Third Reich twenty
years before its birth that its accredited spokesmen
sound as if they are merely obeying Veblen's logic not
only in broad outline but in specific detail." Veblen in-
cludes Japan in his analysis of Germany. See also his
paper "Opportunity of Japan," included in his *Essays
in Our Changing Order*, a posthumous collection of
papers from periodicals, edited by Leon Ardzrooni
(New York, 1934). Of the German people he said in
1915 that "they are not in a position to take up a relation of tutelage to any other community, with the slightest chance of a successful issue, for good or ill. They
are physically, technologically, politically, socially, comprised within the frontiers of modern Christendom; but
they are, in certain indefeasible respects, notably the
industrial respect, newcomers whose scheme of life has
not yet been made over in the image of that culture into
which they are moving by force of unavoidable habituation — unavoidable except by a precipitate retreat into
that more archaic phase of Western civilization out of
which they have latterly been escaping. It is not yet too
late, perhaps. They may yet be able to effect such a
retreat by recourse to so drastic a reaction in their civil
and political institutions as will offset, presently neu-
tralize, and eventually dispel the effects wrought by
habituation to the ways and means of modern industry
and the exact sciences." (*Imperial Germany*, p. 236 f.)
Veblen foresaw that the Germans may yet be able to
effect the drastic retreat from the West.

13. *An Inquiry into the Nature of Peace*, p. 202 f.

14. Alfred Thayer Mahan, *Naval Strategy Compared and Contrasted with the Principles and Practice
of Military Operations on Land* (Boston: Little, Brown,
1911), p. 109.

15. *An Inquiry into the Nature of Peace*, p. 227.

16. *Ibidem*, p. 228 ff.

17. *Ibidem*, p. 231 f. "In the face of such a neutral league Imperial Japan alone would be unable to make a really serious diversion or to entertain much hope of following up its quest of dominion."

18. *Ibidem*, p. 295 f.

19. James Murdoch and Isoh Yamagata, *A History of Japan*, vol. II: "During the Century of Early Foreign Intercourse (1542–1651)" (London: Kegan Paul, 1925), pp. 309–311.

20. Yoshi S. Kuno, *Japanese Expansion on the Asiatic Continent: A Study in the History of Japan with Special Reference to Her International Relations with China, Korea and Russia*, vol. I (Berkeley, Calif.: University of California Press, 1932), p. 313 f.

21. Harley Farnsworth MacNair, *The Real Conflict between China and Japan: An Analysis of Opposing Ideologies* (Chicago: University of Chicago Press, 1938), p. 99. An excellent book for a real understanding of the issues in the Far East.

22. Payson Jackson Treat, *The Early Diplomatic Relations between the United States and Japan, 1853–1865* (Baltimore: Johns Hopkins Press, 1917), p. 99 f.

23. Shinkichi Uyesugi, "Emperor Worship in Japan," English tranlation in *Japan Weekly Chronicle*, June 26, 1913, p. 1172, quoted in Kenneth W. Colegrove, "The Japanese Emperor," I, *The American Political Science Review*, vol. XXVI, no. 4 (August 1932), p. 647. The article in the *American Political Science Review*, XXVI, 642–659, 828–845, and Kenneth W. Colegrove's *Militarism in Japan* (Boston: World Peace Foundation, 1936) contain much relevant material.

24. In *Trans-Pacific* of August 4, 1932, quoted in MacNair, *op. cit.*, pp. 135–136.

25. MacNair, *op. cit.*, p. 183. Baron Kiichiro Hiranuma who was appointed Prime Minister on January 5, 1939, is reported to have said early in 1939, "Japan has

the Heavenly Way and nothing else. Herein lies the secret of state administration. . . . If anyone dares obstruct Japan in the pursuit of this righteous Way, she must resolutely overcome this obstruction. The Japanese people are possessed of the martial spirit and if the other party refuses to listen to reason, recourse must be had to force. Japan is thus a country of the gods, a country of high morality and one in which the martial spirit is held in high regard. . . . Any religion which does not conform with this Way must be rejected." (Quoted by Joe J. Mickle, Jr., "Liberalism in Eclipse," *Southwest Review*, Autumn 1941, p. 118.)

26. Mickle, *loc. cit.*, p. 119.

27. MacNair, *op. cit.*, p. 146 f.

28. MacNair, *op. cit.*, p. 154.

29. "The people are being constantly bombarded with propaganda by the press, the radio, and all possible channels. Nothing in the way of criticism is tolerated. The war in China is not presented as one of conquest and exploitation but rather as a holy crusade to rid that land of unjust rulers, red communists, and inaugurate there a regime of peace, righteousness, and prosperity. Even Christian ministers have come to believe that Japan has a divine commitment to pacify the world, and they regard the army as the chief instrument for this purpose. The alliance with the Fascist nations is constantly being celebrated, and the resources of the empire are being mobilized for undertakings abroad which will require years to complete. And the very fact that divine sanctions are given Japanese conquests makes the problem all the more serious." (MacNair, *op. cit.*, p. 193 f.)

30. Ferdinand Kürnberger, *Der Amerikamüde*, 2nd ed. (Leipzig: Reclam, 1889), p. 211 f. "Was die deutschen Bauern Pennsylvaniens in tiefster Bewusstlosigkeit gewusst haben: deutsches Leben ein Jahrhundert lang festzuhalten, so festzuhalten, dass heute

noch ganze Gemeinden von ihnen kein englisches
Wort verstehen, das sollte ich mit dem begeister-
ten Bewusstsein deutscher Art und Bildung weniger
weittragend zu überliefern vermögen? Ich fürchte es
nicht. Nein, ich werde ausdauern, Deutscher im Yan-
keetum, und der Sturz, den ich diesem Mischvolke
bevorstehen sehe, kann mich so wenig bekümmern, als
uns das Los einer Ziege kümmert, die einen Jupiter
grossgesäugt hat. Mag's dann hereinbrechen, wie diese
Blätter zu prophezeien wagen, wir werden in den Bür-
gerkriegen der Union nicht zu Grunde gehen. Deutschland wird seine Flotte schicken, und seine deutsche
Provinz Pennsylvanien sich zu schützen wissen. Was
sag' ich: Pennsylvanien? Ganz Nordamerika wird
deutsch werden, denn unsre Einwanderung stützt sich
dann auf ein mächtiges Mutterland, sowie sich Yan-
keeenglisch auf Altengland stützte. Aber was sag' ich
ganz Nordamerika? Die ganze Welt wird deutsch werden, denn mit Deutschlands Aufgang wird England
untergehen, wie Holland vor England unterging, und
sämtliche englische Kolonien werden dann dem Deutsch-
tume zufallen . . . die Wachtposten der Kultur werden
auf dem ganzen Erdenrund abgelöst und mit deutscher
Mannschaft bezogen werden. Deutschland erwacht,
und kein Volk der Welt behauptet seinen alten Rang,
denn alle leben vom deutschen Schlafe und verderben
mit deutschem Auferstehen."

This fantasy is of course entirely unrelated to the
earlier plans, advanced often by the liberal German
generation of 1830 and of 1848, of founding in the
United States "a German state which would naturally
become a member of the American Union but which
would maintain a form of government that would guarantee the permanence of German civilization and the
German language and provide for a free and democratic existence," a "rejuvenated Germany in North
America," not in the spirit of the old European Ger-

many, but truly democratic. That was the program developed for instance in 1833 in Giessen in the "Aufforderung und Erklärung in betreff einer Auswanderung im grossen aus Deutschland in die Nordamerikanischen Freistaaten" quoted in John A. Hawgood, *The Tragedy of German-America* (New York: Putnam, 1940), p. 109. But these German immigrants, in spite of their plans, soon became fully Americanized. One of their leaders, Friedrich Münch, wrote on the occasion of the German revolution of 1848: "We almost repented of having given up our Fatherland as hopeless and would willingly have thrown ourselves into the struggle there, but already we and our families had taken deep root in the life of the new world." (*Ibidem*, p. 113 f.)

31. See *Not By Arms Alone*, pp. 3–30.

32. One great German poet and religious thinker who had come deeply under Nietzsche's influence wrote in his diary in 1897: "One looks Nietzsche in the eyes and knows where humanity's goal lies." But in 1912 he wrote: "Is not Nietzsche one of our greatest stylists? And nevertheless he remained sterile in a higher sense. I weigh my words, for if any one has ever experienced Nietzsche, I did it. And not in me was he sterile. But I also know wherein he was for a long time my ideal: in his greatness as a human being, not in his unfortunately only too seasonal (ach nur allzu zeitgemässen) way of philosophy. That was sunset, not dawn, and who attempts to start from it and to progress further, marches into night (und wer von ihr weiterschreitet, der wandelt in die Nacht)." (Christian Morgenstern, *Stufen, Eine Entwicklung in Aphorismen und Tagebuch-Notizen*, Munich: Piper, 1918, pp. 78, 82.)

33. *Mein Kampf* (Munich: Eher, 1933), p. 437 f.

34. Moeller van den Bruck, *Germany's Third Empire*, tr. by E. O. Lorimer (London: Allen & Unwin, 1934), p. 192. Though *Das Dritte Reich* was never widely read even in Germany, it is most characteristic

for the spirit out of which National Socialist Germany arose, not only in its fierce and irreconcilable hostility to all Western thought, to all rationalism, liberalism, and catholicism, but also in its feelings of the approaching apocalypse, in which Germany will play the decisive role, because the German nation cannot be compared with any other nation. Other nations aspire to create states, the German nation, the Reich. "Der deutsche Nationalismus ist Streiter für das Endreich. Es ist die besondere Verheissung des deutschen Volkes, die ihm alle anderen Völker streitig machen. Aber . . . es gibt nur Ein Reich, wie es nur Eine Kirche gibt. Es gibt nur Das Reich. Der deutsche Nationalismus kämpft für das mögliche Reich. Der deutsche Nationalist dieser Zeit ist als deutscher Mensch immer noch ein Mystiker, aber als politischer Mensch ist er Skeptiker geworden." (Moeller van den Bruck, *Das Dritte Reich*, third ed., Hamburg: Hanseatische Verlagsanstalt, 1931, p. 244 f.) This fusion of an absolute mysticism with an absolute skepticism has become characteristic of National Socialism. In the Western countries civilization was at the same time corroded by a similar, though less profound, skepticism, but with no mysticism.

35. Otto Gierke, *Political Theories of the Middle Age*, tr. by Frederick William Maitland (Cambridge University Press, 1913), p. 81.

36. Nothing announced the approaching decomposition and fall of France as clearly as the spirit, or rather lack of spirit, with which in 1939 the one hundred and fiftieth anniversary of the French Revolution and of the Declaration of the Rights of Man was celebrated, if it was not, and that intentionally, forgotten as something better not mentioned. On January 5, 1940, the old Belgian liberal statesman, Paul Hymans, pointed out before an audience in the University of Brussels the importance of the Declaration: "Elle conserve à cent cinquante ans de distance, un magnifique rayonnement. On trouve en

elle l'esprit de l'Amérique nouvelle, l'esprit liberal de la vieille Angleterre, l'esprit genial d'une France soudainement affranchie, redressée, dont la parole remuera l'Europe. Les auteurs de la Déclaration des Droits ont voulu, disent-ils eux-mêmes, parler pour tous les hommes, pour tous les temps. La Déclaration n'est pas un formulaire philosophique ni un manifeste révolutionnaire. C'est le programme de la vie sociale et politique des peuples civilisés, arrivés après une longue évolution au niveau de culture politique et morale nécessaire pour se gouverner eux-mêmes, capables d'une liberté intelligente, tolerante et disciplinée, qui suscite l'effort et la concurrence, proscrit le privilège et l'arbitraire, et féconde le travail de la pensée, l'art et la technique." (Quoted in *La France Libre*, 15 November 1941, p. 21.)

37. "Alle Gerechtigkeit ist in irgend einem Sinne Gleichbehandlung," Hans Nef, *Gleichheit und Gerechtigkeit* (Zurich: Polygraphischer Verlag, 1941). Göring called in a speech before the Academy for German Law in November 1934 the concept of equality "the sworn enemy" of National Socialism (*Reden und Aufsätze*, Munich: Eher, 1938, p. 144).

38. Alfred Cobban, *op. cit.*, p. 86. "Now the only alternative to absolute sovereignty or the rule of arbitrary will, is law. It has sometimes been said in recent years that what the world needs is a revival of authority. This is an error: there is no lack of authority in the world today, but contemporary evidence proves only too clearly that the revival of authority is not the same thing as the return of law and may even be its opposite." (*Ibidem*, p. 85.) "The effect of recreating a belief in Natural Law, which is ethical law, would be to make it possible to reëstablish positive law, and with it government and society, on a basis of right" (*Ibidem*, p. 134).

39. In spite of all their similarities, there exist differences between National Socialism and Fascism, though with the growing preponderance of National Socialism

and the effacement of Fascism they become less and less discernible, not so much in the attitude of the peoples (how different the reaction of the Italian people to Fascism has been compared with that of the German people to National Socialism has been clearly shown in this war) as in theory. Fascism was, at the beginning, much more a technique for the conquest of power than a doctrine. In National Socialism the doctrine prevailed, though it contained also elements of technique of conquest. The logical and metaphysical mind of the Germans has brought all the elements potentially inherent in Fascism to their extreme and total manifestation, while in Italy and France they remain partially cloaked by compromise and a remnant of common sense, by slackness as well as by the saving grace of humor. The authoritarianism of Fascism is more conservative, and in men like Marshal Pétain or General Franco turned toward the Middle Ages and not to a complete transvaluation of all values. The Roman Catholic Church could therefore hope to make its peace with Fascism, it never could with National Socialism. Fascism in all Latin countries has been accommodating to the Church, perhaps partly, as in the case of Charles Maurras, because of its largely irreligious character. National Socialism is too much of a totalitarian religion itself to accommodate the Church. And there is another difference: when Fascism glorifies the past of Italy, it finds there the universal Rome of the Caesars and the universal Rome of the Popes, both bearers of Western civilization. National Socialism, looking to Germany's past, glorifies there the eternal revolt against the West, Arminius against the Romans, the Saxons against Charlemagne, Luther against Rome. National Socialism draws its main inspiration from the German struggle against "alien" universal values, and even beyond it from prehistoric tribal times.

40. Few events of the past years were as indicative

of the crisis as the corruption of pacifism, which — entirely legitimate as a religious pattern of life, as a witness through sacrifice and martyrdom, and as such a witness a salt of the earth and a reminder of the verities — began to cater to the egotism and hedonism of the people, promising them peace and happiness if only they would not go to war for their fellow men. Thus pacifism, through helping to dull the understanding of the present situation and undermining the will to intelligent and timely resistance and the necessary preparation for it, objectively helped Chancellor Hitler's and the Japanese plans of aggression. By a supreme irony the pacifists thus helped the most anti-pacific force on earth. From this point it was only a slight step to a pacifism asserting that Hitler really meant peace, in a more or less veiled way accepting most of his pretexts and excuses, and finally justifying the Germans and finding faults with their victims. The principle of non-resistance to evil is a great principle if men carry it out, listening only to the voice within themselves, and ready to bear all martyrdom for its sake. It becomes something entirely different if it is transferred to the political scene, over the radio and in mass-meetings, not in an absolute earnestness, but in an argument as to the time when a nation should defend itself, whether in an un-Christian egotism when its own frontiers are invaded, or wisely and courageously helping fellow victims of aggression. The principle of non-resistance to evil degenerated into a denial that evil exists, into an appeal to accept the evil and to condone injustice. Thus pacifism, instead of bearing witness to the verities, became in the universal crisis one of the elements which could be used and abused by the aggressor nations for the destruction of the verities.

41. *The War Diary of the Emperor Frederick III 1870–1871*, translated by A. R. Allinson (London: Stanley Paul, 1927), p. 240.

42. "The war began in the soul of the English people. This is a people's war if there ever was one. How ironic that those who are forever talking about a people's this and a people's that should have been stopped from seeing a real people's movement when it appeared. This war started as a murmur low down where common men live. It became an outcry and ultimately a roar. . . . Some of us have loathed war as a chief iniquity, yet this war represents the cleanest and finest thing we have seen the English people do. . . . Hitler becomes the occasioning and releasing cause of the whitest flame of life we have yet seen. In all this we see how inadequate were our shallow philosophies of history." (Clifford L. Stanley, "Russia and the War," *Christianity and Society*, vol. VII, 1942, no. 1, p. 15.)

43. Ksawery Pruszyński wrote in *Wiadomości Polskie* (London, Jan. 12, 1941): "The Polish nation is at present passing through a period of very intensive thinking and reappraisal from the bottom up of the things it believes in and trusts. I dare say that so powerful a process of thinking about our own concerns we have experienced only twice before: in the Reformation period of the 16th century and later in the period just before the Partition when the Four Years' Diet was in session." (Quoted by Arthur P. Coleman in *Journal of Central European Affairs*, vol. I, January 1942, p. 400.)

44. *New York Times*, Dec. 25, 1940, p. 1.

45. On June 15, 1941, Toshio Shiratori, the advisor of the Japanese Foreign Office, wrote: "The greatest reason for Japan's participation in the Triple Alliance lies in the fact that the three signatory powers, at this time of great change in the world situation, have the same position, the same interest, and entertain the same political views. China is not Japan's real enemy in the present incident. In reality Japan is fighting Britain and America. The first thing we are now required to do is to carry out our southward advance. When Europe and

Asia are placed under the new order, America will be unable to maintain her capitalism."

46. See *New York Times*, Jan. 3, 1942, on Dr. Alfred Rosenberg's tenets of the religion of National Socialism. The thirty-point program of the National Reich Church limits the Church to the frontiers of the Reich and its colonies. "Other churches or religious associations, above all those based on international bodies or directed from abroad, will not be tolerated in Germany." "The National Reich Church is immutably fixed in its one objective: to destroy that Christian belief imported into Germany in the unfortunate year 800, whose tenets conflict with both the heart and the mentality of the Germans."

47. Associated Press dispatch from Berlin, Nov. 30, 1941. See *New York Herald Tribune*, Dec. 1, 1941. An Associated Press dispatch from Rome, Nov. 10, 1941, published in the *New York Times* of Nov. 11, 1941, reports a broadcast from the Vatican of a catechism, published in the German weekly *Nordland*, organ of the German Believers in God, of Sept. 15. According to the Vatican report the catechism contained among others the following statement: "The divine manifests itself in the cosmos, in nature inanimate and animate. . . . The divine in the highest form is personified in the (German) people. . . . It derives from it that service for the Führer, for the people and for the fatherland is divine service." "To believe in our people and its mission means: 1. To have unshakable conviction that our people represents the highest worth of all humanity on earth. 2. To follow the will of nature according to which the best people is called upon to command. 3. To know that to be led by the best people redounds from the necessity of things in benediction on other nations. 4. To work, sacrifice ourselves and fight indefatigably for the ascent and victory of our people." From the original German text of *Gott und Volk* the *Neue Volkszeitung*,

New York, Feb. 28, 1942, quoted: "Zweitausend Jahre lang . . . hat die christliche Kirche Zeit gehabt, die Menschheit in eine reinere und höherstrebende Rasse umzuwandeln. Die christliche Kirche aber hat das nicht nur unterlassen, sondern ist zu einem Hindernis einer solchen Entwicklung geworden. Endlich ist Adolf Hitler erschienen, um Gottes wahren Willen zu erkennen und zu gestalten. Weil das Christentum versagt hat, hat nun seine Todesstunde geschlagen. . . . Die Fronten sind klar geschieden. Man ist entweder ein Christ oder man ist ein Deutscher. Ein Drittes gibt es nicht. . . . Das christliche Kreuz und das deutsche Schwert sind miteinander unvereinbar. Das deutsche Volk erwacht. . . . Das Bild des Gekreuzigten wird verschwinden. Der Held unsres Glaubens hält das Schwert in der Faust und trägt nicht das Kreuz auf dem Rücken. Der ewige Mahner des neuen deutschen Glaubens ist nicht der Gekreuzigte, sondern der unbekannte Soldat, der im Kriege gefallen ist. Er und alle Deutschen, die noch fallen werden — das sind unsere Heiligen. Für katholische Prozessionen, für Reliquienglauben und den orientalischen Sünden-Komplex aber ist kein Raum mehr. Wir müssen wieder ein Soldatenvolk werden, Soldaten des Krieges und der Arbeit. . . . Man kann zwar beten, aber man stammelt nicht Bitten, feige, wie es der Christ tut. Man bittet nicht um Gnade und Barmherzigkeit. Das Gebet des Deutschen besteht in innerer Zucht und Disziplin, in einem feierlichen Versprechen, in einem ehrfürchtigen Aufblicken zum Bildnis des Führers oder zur Fahne."

48. This fact explains the Vatican's refusal to back National Socialism and the National Socialist "crusade" against communism. Against fascist expectations, the Pope did not mention the war against the Soviet Union in his broadcast on Sunday June 29, 1941, one week after Chancellor Hitler launched his attack against the Soviet Union. The *Osservatore Romano* of Feb. 15,

1941, published a strong denial of a story that the Pontiff takes the anti-democratic side (*New York Times*, Feb. 16, 1941). On Jan. 21, 1942, the *Osservatore Romano* denied that the status of the Catholic Church in Germany was reassuring. It reprinted a statement which had originally appeared on July 4, 1941: "However much it may irk the Axis powers, the Catholic Church will continue to express its determination to defend the right of peoples to liberty, which it considers one of the fundamental conditions of equitable peace. Liberty, moreover is considered by the Church to be a natural law without which there can be neither personality nor responsibility." (*New York Times*, Jan. 22, 1942.) The attitude of the Vatican is not identical with that of the Catholic priests in Italy. Most of them are more Italian Fascists than Catholics. But Italian Catholics have given rise to such a truly Catholic movement as that of Don Luigi Sturzo.

49. In this National Socialist morale the asceticism and rigorism of the Teutonic Knights lives on. Its best recent representative was perhaps Walter Flex, who fell in the First World War and whose novel *Der Wanderer zwischen beiden Welten* (1916) was the most widely read war book of the German youth. See William K. Pfeiler, *War and the German Mind* (New York: Columbia University Press, 1941), pp. 82–90, and especially S. D. Stirk, *The Prussian Spirit. A Survey of German Literature and Politics 1914–1940* (London: Faber, 1941), pp. 78–82. Flex wrote the popular poem "Preussische Fahneneid" which culminates in the lines

"Wer auf die preussische Fahne schwört,
  Hat nichts mehr, was ihm selber gehört."
  ("Whoever takes the oath to the Prussian flag,
  No longer possesses anything that belongs to himself.")

But more characteristic of the present attitude than Flex, who was still a Prussian of the nineteenth century, is

Ernst Jünger, whose ideal type is the completely mechanized and permanently mobilized man who is worker and soldier at the same time. What Marx had foreseen as a possibility in his *Communist Manifesto* when he wrote of modern industry that "masses of workers, crowded together in the factory, are organized in military fashion," has been brought to its logical extreme in Jünger's *Die totale Mobilmachung* (1931), which, like his *Der Arbeiter: Herrschaft und Gestalt* (2nd ed., Hamburg: Hanseatische Verlagsanstalt, 1932), presents the most perfect synthesis of Prussianism and industrial technology, something which Oswald Spengler had in mind when he wrote his *Preussentum und Sozialismus*. In his war book *Wäldchen 125* (English translation *Copse 125*, London: Chatto & Windus, 1929) he wrote about the coming German nationalism: "Der behördlich wohl geregelte Patriotismus ebensowohl wie die Kräfte, die sich ihm gegenüberstellen, müssen von einem dämonisch aus allen Schichten auflodernden Glauben an Volk und Vaterland verschlungen werden, jeder anders Fühlende muss mit dem Brandmal des Ketzers behaftet und ausgerottet werden. Wir können gar nicht national genug sein. Eine Revolution, die das auf ihre Fahnen schreibt, soll uns stets in ihren Reihen finden. . . . Die Gliederung aller Deutschen in das grosse Hundertmillionenreich der Zukunft, das ist ein Ziel, für das es sich wohl zu sterben und jeden Widerstand niederzuschlagen lohnt." (The kind of patriotism which is carefully directed into certain channels by the authorities, as well as the forces which oppose patriotism, must be swallowed up by a belief in the *Volk* and the Fatherland which with demon-like power flares up from all classes of society; everybody who feels differently must be branded with the mark of the heretic and exterminated. We cannot possibly be nationalist enough. A revolution which inscribes this on its banners must and will always find us in its ranks. . . . The merging of all Germans into the great empire of a hundred millions which the future will bring — that is an aim for which it is worth while to die and to beat down all opposition.) See also *Not By Arms Alone*, p. 11.

50. "Grundsätzlich: Unser nationalsozialistisches Program setzt an Stelle des liberalistischen Begriffes des Individuums, des marxistischen Begriffes der Menschheit das blutbedingte und mit dem Boden verbundene Volk. Ein sehr einfacher und lapidarer Satz, allein von gewaltigen Auswirkungen. Zum erstenmal vielleicht, seit es eine Menschengeschichte gibt, ist in diesem Lande die Erkenntnis dahin gelenkt worden, dass von allen Aufgaben, die uns gestellt sind, die erhabenste und damit für den Menschen heiligste die Erhaltung der von Gott gegebenen blutgebundenen Art ist." (*Frankfurter Zeitung*, Jan. 31, 1937.) In the same address Hitler points out the consequences of the fundamental principle for the concept of law. Law becomes subservient to racial purposes. On September 6, 1938, at Nürnberg, Alfred Rosenberg delivered a discourse against the Roman Catholic Church in which he said: "The racial doctrine has been characterized as an element of discord, of spiritual separatism and of fanaticism, of barbarism and of the return to bestialism. In their attacks against the racial doctrine these philosophico-religious institutions (the Church and the Papacy) entered into an alliance with atheist Marxism, which they pretend to combat, but of which they share in reality the universalist attitude."

51. Alfred Rosenberg, *Der Mythus des 20. Jahrhunderts* (Munich: Hoheneichen-Verlag, 1934), p. 458: "Katholizismus, Protestantismus, Judentum, Naturalismus müssen vor einer neuen Weltanschauung das Feld räumen, so dass ihrer nicht mehr gedacht werde, wie der Nachtlampe nicht mehr gedacht wird, wenn die Morgensonne über die Berge scheint — oder aber die Einheit Deutschlands wird von Tag zu Tag fraglicher."

52. Rosenberg, *op. cit.*, p. 675, saw as the goal of the historical development a political system which would safeguard the political domination of the white race over the globe. To that end he suggested, on p. 676, an alliance of the Nordic bloc (Germany and Scandinavia) with England which would make Great Britain's domination of India secure. The book was first published in 1930, though the author claims in the preface that it was practically completed in 1925.

53. Karl Rosenfelder, "Die Abkehr der Romkirche von Europa," *Nationalsozialistische Monatshefte*, 104 (November 1938), p. 947. He pits against the "lebensfeindlichen, völkerzerstörenden Ideen der Freimaurerei, des Judentums, des Marxismus und der Romkirche den Gedanken des nordischen Wesens." "Zu den grossen internationalen geistigen Mächten, die einer nordisch bestimmten weissen Völkergemeinschaft unversöhnlich gegenüberstehen, gehört auch die Romkirche."

54. Rosenberg, *op. cit.*, pp. 678–681, "Das Ende des Bonifazius." "Odin als das ewige Spiegelbild der seelischen Urkräfte des nordischen Menschen lebt heute wie vor 5000 Jahren."

55. Rosenberg, *op. cit.*, p. 155. "Heute ist es jedem aufrichtigen Deutschen klar, dass mit dieser alle Geschöpfe der Welt gleichmässig umfassenden Liebeslehre ein empfindlicher Schlag gegen die Seele des nordischen Europas geführt worden ist."

56. Rosenberg, *op. cit.*, p. 204. "Wir sehen hier im Marxismus die Idee des Opfers und der 'Liebe' die gleiche Rolle spielen, wie im römischen System."

57. Pope Pius XI pointed out in a decree of the Congregation of the Holy Office on March 21, 1928, that the Church "ita vel maxime damnat odium adversus populum olim a Deo electum, odium nempe illud, quod vulgo 'antisemitismi' nomine nunc significari solet." In an address before the students of the College of Propaganda at the Vatican, Pope Pius, who spoke in French,

discussed on July 28, 1938, the implications of racialism and nationalism from the Catholic point of view: "Catholique veut dire universel, non pas raciste, non pas nationaliste dans le sens separatiste des deux adjectifs. . . . Nous ne voulons séparer rien dans la famille humaine. Nous considérons le racisme et le nationalisme comme des barrières érigées entre homme et homme, nation et nation. . . . On oublie que le genre humain, tout le genre humain est une seule, grande et universelle race humaine. . . . La réalité humaine consiste dans le fait que ce sont des hommes, non pas des fauves ou des êtres quelconques; la dignité humaine consiste en ceci: que tous font une seule grande famille, le genre humain, la race humaine." On September 6, 1938, Pope Pius XI received a pilgrimage of Belgian teachers; thumbing through a missal before him he paused at the passage commemorating the sacrifice of Abraham at the most solemn moment of the mass. "Sacrificium Patriarchae Nostri Abrahae," he read and commented: "Notice that Abraham is called our patriarch, our ancestor. Antisemitism is incompatible with the sublime thought and reality which are expressed in this text. . . . Through Christ and in Christ, we are all spiritual descendants of Abraham. . . . We are spiritually Semites."

58. See *Revolutions and Dictatorships*, pp. 240–253; *Not By Arms Alone*, pp. 105–123.

59. "At a certain moment the era of ferocious nationalisms will disappear, as suddenly as the religious wars ended in Europe three centuries ago" (Count Carlo Sforza, *The Totalitarian War and After*, Chicago: University of Chicago Press, 1941).

60. Hans Kohn, *History of Nationalism in the East* (London: Routledge, 1929), pp. 6, 122, 128 f., 377, 386.

61. The story of Eboué is told in Denis Saurat, *Watch over Africa* (London: Dent, 1941).

62. The Soviet-Polish declaration of friendship of

December 4, 1941, reads: "The Government of the Soviet Union and the Government of the Polish Republic, motivated by a spirit of friendly agreement and military coöperation, declare: 1. German Hitlerite Imperialism is the most evil enemy of mankind. It is impossible to make any compromise with it. Both Governments, together with Great Britain and other allies, and with the support of the United States of America, will continue the war until complete victory and the final destruction of the German invaders. 2. In putting into operation the agreement signed in June 1941, both Governments will lend each other full military aid during the war. The forces of the Polish Government on Soviet territory will conduct the fight against the German robbers shoulder to shoulder with the Soviet forces. In peace time the basis of mutual relations will be good-neighbourly collaboration, friendship and the carrying out of obligations agreed upon. 3. After the victorious termination of the war and the suitable punishment of the German criminals, the task of the Allied Governments will be to guarantee a just and enduring peace. This can only be achieved by a new organization of international relations based on an enduring alliance between the democratic countries. In the creation of such an organization a vital condition will be respect for international law supported by the collective armed forces of all Allied countries. Only under such conditions can the Europe destroyed by the German barbarians be resurrected and a guarantee given that the catastrophe now occurring in Europe will not be repeated."

63. In an article, "The Federation of the World," reprinted in *International Conciliation*, no. 342, September 1938, p. 326. In the same year Mr. Holt used the term in an article, "The United States Peace Commission," *North American Review*, September 1910. The expression seems to have been first suggested by Mr. Hayne Davis in 1903.

64. The Joint Resolution was passed unanimously by the House on March 11, 1941, and by a vote of 45 to 5 in the Senate on March 12, 1941, and signed by the Speaker and Lieutenant Governor on March 13, 1941. Printed in *International Conciliation*, no. 371, June 1941. It was the third and most explicit resolution of this kind by legislative bodies in the United States. Previously the House of Representatives and the Senate of the United States had passed unanimously, in June 1910, House Joint Resolution 223, authorizing the appointment of a Commission in Relation to Universal Peace and suggesting "constituting the combined navies of the world an international force for the preservation of universal peace." The House of Representatives and the Senate of the Commonwealth of Massachusetts passed a resolution in February 1915 requesting Congress to invite all the nations to unite in the formation of a world state. The Resolution declared: "The United States of America affirms the political unity of all mankind. It affirms the supremacy of world sovereignty over national sovereignty. It promises loyal obedience to that sovereignty."

SOME RECENT BOOKS

SOME RECENT BOOKS

THE FOLLOWING LIST of books confines itself to some of the very recent publications which may help to elucidate the problems connected with the world crisis and its manifestations in the present war and with the issues confronting us after the war. It represents a continuation of the three bibliographies given in *Revolutions and Dictatorships* (first printing, 1939), *Not By Arms Alone* (1940) and *Revolutions and Dictatorships* (second printing, 1941).

BENEDETTO CROCE, *History as the Story of Liberty* (New York: Norton, 1941).

The aged Italian philosopher who has lived for twenty years under fascist domination maintains that liberty is an imperishable "moral idea" and not merely a "contingent fact." "Liberty has lived, and will always live in history, a perilous and fighting life."

ALFRED COBBAN, *Crisis of Civilization* (London: Jonathan Cape, 1941).

A remarkable and thought-provoking book on the foundations of civilization. "The whole of this book has been written to no purpose if it is not realized that rights are rights for actual living men and women, and not for the buried generations of the past or the unguessable future." "It is often said that the mis-

takes of the League were, first that it was not universal, and secondly that it expected too much of its
members. But the weakness of the League was due to
its undue extension and its fear of infringing in any
way the sovereignty of its members. The attempt to
run it as a cross between the Student Christian Movement and a limited liability company, the shareholders
in which invested an infinitesimal capital and expected a large interest and full security, could not but
fail. Any future league must begin by aiming at
strength and not at universality."

CHARLES E. MERRIAM, *What is Democracy?* Chicago:
University of Chicago Press, 1941).
Democracy "is not dependent upon any economic system. . . . It is not the property of the white or the
black or the brown race. It is not the possession of
Aryans or non-Aryans." It asumes the "dignity of
man and the importance of treating personalities upon
a fraternal rather than a differential basis."

FREDERICK L. SCHUMAN, *International Politics. The
Western State System in Transition* (Third edition.
New York: McGraw-Hill, 1941).
Though the book is intended primarily as a textbook,
it is of interest to the general reader as a comprehensive survey of the problems of world order and world
anarchy.

D. W. BROGAN, *Is Innocence Enough?* (London: Hamish Hamilton, 1941).
Most thoughtful and pertinent though not always
connected reflections on foreign affairs.

A. BERRIEDALE KEITH, *The Causes of the War* (London:
Nelson, 1940).
In this detailed and highly interesting volume the
well-known student of Indian literature and of the
constitutional law of the British Empire examines
carefully the diplomatic scene of the world before the

outbreak of this war and down to the formation of
the Churchill government.

PAUL BIRDSALL, *Versailles Twenty Years Later* (New
York: Reynal & Hitchcock, 1941).

A highly readable and scholarly book with an excellent analysis of Versailles diplomacy. "By a curious
logic the inevitable European chaos which resulted
from American isolation has been used as a further
foundation for isolationist argument. . . . The complete distortion of the role of the United States in the
first World War and at Versailles crystallized a powerful isolationist sentiment which threatened to para-
lyze American foreign policy in the present increasingly critical world situation."

DWIGHT E. LEE, *Ten Years: The World On Its Way to
War 1930–1940* (Boston: Houghton Mifflin, 1942).

A detailed survey of the fateful decade.

PAUL EINZIG, *Appeasement Before, During and After
Munich* (London: Macmillan, 1941).

An important analysis of appeasement as a policy with
important conclusions not only for waging this war,
but for the period after the war.

HENRY M. WRISTON, *Prepare For Peace!* (New York:
Harper, 1941).

"The spiritual poverty of the isolationists lay in their
lack of faith. Thus they denied and destroyed the
expansive power of the idea of freedom. Nothing but
feebleness of faith in a great ideal would have yielded
the initiative wholly into the hands of the exponents
of an ignoble escape from individual responsibility.
When Mussolini proclaimed he would trample the
'rotting carcass of liberty,' it was the inevitable response to the isolationist retreat from responsibility."

VICOUNT CECIL, *A Real Peace* (London: Hamish Hamilton, 1941).

Important suggestions by the old fighter for peace.

His remarkable autobiography, *A Great Experiment* (London: Jonathan Cape, 1941), ends with the words: "No machinery can do more than facilitate the action of the peoples. Unless they and their governments really put the enforcement of the law and the maintenance of peace as the first and greatest of national interests, no federation can compel them to do so. But I believe that federation, the constitutional union of independent states, inside the general framework of the League may help to make men realize that it is only by international coöperation that peace can be preserved."

HAROLD BUTLER, *The Lost Peace. A Personal Impression* (London: Faber, 1941).

By the former deputy director and director of the International Labor Office. Moderate in its views and charitable in its judgments. "No country, when it came to the point, was ready to pledge the lives of its soldiers 'in other people's quarrels.' . . . If peace is really indivisible, will not some world organization like the League of Nations still be necessary?"

FORREST DAVIS, *The Atlantic System* (New York: Reynal & Hitchcock, 1941).

The story of Anglo-American control of the seas with an important discussion of America's foreign policy and its possible implications.

H. R. KNICKERBOCKER, *Is Tomorrow Hitler's?* (New York: Reynal & Hitchcock, 1941).

Though this book was published in the fall of 1941, its sharp and incisive answers to the questions uppermost in the minds of most Americans retain their full validity.

HAROLD J. LASKI, *The Strategy of Freedom: An Open Letter to American Youth* (New York: Harper, 1941).

An analysis of the issues of the present war and their significance for America and for freedom.

RALPH BARTON PERRY, *On All Fronts* (New York: Vanguard Press, 1941).

"The popular appeal of isolationism lies in the fact that it lets men off; it gives them a reprieve which they readily mistake for acquittal." "Hemispheric isolationism is no better than national isolationism. Mankind does not divide into hemispheres."

EDWARD MEAD EARLE, *Against This Torrent* (Princeton: Princeton University Press, 1941).

One of the best short studies on American foreign policy in the present war. Though the events have partly taken care of some of the problems, a careful study of American foreign policy and of the attitude of the people before December 7, 1941, remains most essential to an understanding of the issues and to a successful conduct of the war and of the peace.

W. F. KERNAN, *Defense Will Not Win the War* (Boston: Little, Brown, 1942).

A very much needed restatement of the fallacies which have dominated American thought and a discussion of the strategy needed for survival and victory.

FRITZ BURI, *Christentum und Kultur bei Albert Schweitzer. Eine Einführung in sein Denken als Weg zu einer christlichen Weltanschauung* (Bern: Paul Haupt, 1941).

Schweitzer's effort at a synthesis of Christianity and civilization, as published in his *Verfall und Wiederaufbau der Kultur* and his *Kultur und Ethik* immediately after the First World War, still retains its fundamental importance. "Nur darauf kommt es an, dass wir den Gedanken des durch sittliche Arbeit zu schaffenden Reiches mit derselben Vehemenz denken, mit der Jesus den von göttlicher Intervention zu erwartenden in sich bewegte, und miteinander wissen, dass wir imstande sein müssen, alles dafür hinzugeben." "Dass Jesus eine übernatürlich sich realisierende Endvollendung erwartet, während wir sie nur als Resultat der sittlichen Arbeit begreifen können, ist mit dem Wandel in dem Vorstellungsmaterial gegeben." "Nur was aus dem Denken geboren, sich an das Denken wendet, kann eine geistige Macht für die ganze Menschheit werden. Nur was in dem Denken der Vielen wiedergedacht und dabei als Wahrheit erfasst wird, besitzt natürlich mitteilbare und dauernde Überzeugungskraft."

KARL BARTH, *A Letter to Great Britain from Switzerland* (London: The Sheldon Press, 1941).

Karl Barth, the leading Protestant theologian, speaks out again to the problems of this war. The pamphlet contains in addition to his Letter to Great Britain his two Letters to the French Protestants. This Letter should be read in conjunction with Barth's earlier writings *Church and State* (London: Student Christian Movement Press, 1939) and *The Church and the Political Problem of Our Day* (New York: Scribner, 1939). This war "is a large-scale police measure which has become absolutely necessary in order to repulse an active anarchism which has become a principle."

NATHANIEL MICKLEM, *The Theology of Politics* (London: Oxford University Press, 1941).

"The communis sensus of mankind, the sacred, the humane and the rational are kindred notions; these are the lamps of civilization; these afford the first principles of politics."

ISACQUE GRAEBER AND STEUART HENDERSON BRITT (Editors), *Jews in a Gentile World* (New York: Macmillan, 1942).

A valuable discussion of the problems of anti-Semitism by American scholars, Christian and Jewish.

KOPPEL S. PINSON (Editor). *Essays on Antisemitism* (New York: Conference on Jewish Relations, 1942). Important and objective historical and analytical studies on anti-Semitism.

ROHAN D'O. BUTLER, *The Roots of National Socialism 1783–1933* (London: Faber, 1941).

Probably the best single volume on the intellectual background of National Socialism. The last chapter called "Foreground" is the most adequate brief summary of the present German mind. "Now it appears how German thought has solved man's painful problem of the right ordering of human life in society. It has solved it in that it has denied it. Harking back by way of the particular and the subjective, through history and thence to superstition, German thought has come to deny the very value of human life within the concord of oecumenical society, holding that right order is only to be achieved by cultivation of the brutishness of tribal man and his worship of the tribal totem."

PETER VIERECK, *Metapolitics. From the Romantics to Hitler* (New York: Knopf, 1941).

An analysis of forerunners and thinkers of National Socialism, especially of Father Jahn, Richard Wagner, and Alfred Rosenberg. Nazi speeches are "fascinating in their pathology, and genuinely impressive and awe-inspiring in their frank revolt against two thousand years of civilization." "What Hitler deems the 'new' religious force of nazism is the oldest of all forces. It is not so much anti-Christian as pre-Christian, as old as Cain, as old as the terrible starkness of nature before Christianity came to tame and restrain nature." See the review in *The Nation*, October 11, 1941.

H. G. ATKINS, *German Literature through Nazi Eyes* (London: Methuen, 1941).

The revaluation of German literature by the National Socialists, by the professor emeritus of German in the University of London.

CRANE BRINTON, *Nietzsche* (Cambridge, Mass.: Harvard University Press, 1941).

See the review in *Annals of American Academy of Political and Social Science*, May 1941, p. 206.

W. W. COOLE AND M. F. POTTER (Editors), *Thus Speaks Germany* (New York: Harper, 1942).

An anthology of German writings, well-documented, but one-sided, with an introduction by Hamilton Fish Armstrong.

F. W. FOERSTER, *Europe and the German Question* (New York: Sheed & Ward, 1940).

A penetrating analysis not alone of Germany but above all of the illusions of a certain pacifism. See also the review by E. J. Knapton, in *The New Commonwealth Quarterly*, vol. VII, no. 1 (July 1941), pp. 25–35. "German propaganda, as it has become more completely the servant of the powers of destruction, has pursued four distinct aims. The first of these is to conceal the attitude behind it and to disguise its mischievous activities as a policy of peace, justice and order. In the second place, it wins over the moral, honorable and peace-loving elements in foreign countries by insincere appeals to their ideals and traditions. In the third place, it also addresses itself to the worst and most unprincipled elements, and by bribery, incitement to violence, and every species of underhand alliance and profit-sharing, attempts to make them conscious or unconscious accomplices of Germany's designs. And in the fourth place, by threats of the alarming consequences of opposing Germany, it spreads the belief that it will be the wisest course to yield to her demands. The employment of these methods achieved such great successes, because the world has been blind to the effectiveness of mental weapons and has treated them as something remote from the world of political realities, as though only visible objects counted for anything."

WILLIAM K. PFEILER, *War and the German Mind. The Testimony of Men of Fiction Who Fought at the*

Front (New York: Columbia University Press, 1941).

An analysis of the German reaction to war as presented in the novels written during the First World War and under its influence.

HERMANN RAUSCHNING, *The Conservative Revolution* (New York: Putnam, 1941).

"For a Western European it is not easy to perceive under the Soviet regime the lines of an individual form of democracy. I admit that I had difficulty myself in realizing them. But it must in fairness be admitted that the Soviet Union shows within its Westernizing development all the elements of our civilization." "The Jewish strain is nothing more and nothing less than one of the German strains, with the special characteristics of the Germans, just as many other of our German strains. There can thus be no other 'settlement' for the future than that the Jewish German is and always will be a German, just as the Bavarian German is. I do regard assimilation as the obvious course. Assimilation does not mean that every distinctive trait must entirely disappear." Many interesting and thought-provoking remarks on Nazism, Marxism, and Prussianism.

HERMANN RAUSCHNING, *The Redemption of Democracy* (New York: Alliance, 1941).

"National Socialism is the most wily and consistent attempt in world history to render the evil in man and the evil man politically useful. Something resembling a world conspiracy of all the criminal instincts and forces in man is now arising. In comparison with the other totalitarian regimes National Socialism is the one really dangerous enemy of human society. It is 'the other' — complete nothingness, the absolute negation of the Western World, of civilization." See the review in *Decision*, April 1941, p. 64.

"Verrina," *The German Mentality* (London: Allen & Unwin, 1941).

Written by a German who regards National Socialism as the culmination of currents long existent in German life and points out that since 1919 Germany has lived increasingly as a parasitic organism on the economic and financial structure of Europe and America.

Edith Roper and Clara Leiser, *Skeleton of Justice* (New York: Dutton, 1941).

Ernst Fraenkel, *The Dual State* (New York: Oxford University Press, 1941).

This book and the preceding one report on the administration of justice in Germany and throw an interesting light on the deterioration of all legal concepts and standards in National Socialist Germany.

Gregor Ziemer, *Education for Death* (New York: Oxford University Press, 1941).

First-hand observations by an American educator of education in Germany and of the mentality of the Nazi youth. A most revealing document, with many quotations from recent original sources.

Allan Nevins, *This Is England Today* (New York: Scribners, 1941).

By the well-known American historian who has spent one year teaching in England during war-time. "Great Britain is in a state of profound and far-reaching upheaval. From top to bottom society is being transformed. The social and economic reorganization is being carried through with more than Spartan fortitude — with self-sacrificing cheerfulness. The war has changed and reshaped every life in the island. It has given Britain already a larger democracy and a truer fraternization." "The essential point is that as great wealth is being abolished, so genuine want is being made impossible."

Geoffrey Mander, *We Were Not All Wrong* (London: Gollancz, 1941).

A vindication of "those members of all parties who foresaw and foretold the war, pointed out in good time the methods by which it might be avoided, and were always willing to provide the physical means for making their ideals prevail."

Lewis Broad, *Winston Churchill* (London: Hutchinson, 1941).

Probably so far the best biography of Churchill, though still very far from being a definitive biography or an approach to it.

J. E. Sewell, *Mirror of England* (London: Hodder & Stoughton, 1941).

An observant journalist reports on the meetings and temper of the British Parliament in 1939 and 1940. In a most handy form important source material is offered by the *Penguin Hansard*, House of Commons Debates, Vol. 1, *From Chamberlain to Churchill*; Vol. 2, *The National Effort*; Vol. 3, *Britain Gathers Strength* (Penguin Books, 1940, 1941).

Joyce Cary, *The Case for African Freedom* (London: Secker & Warburg, 1941).

Margery Perham, *Africans and British Rule* (London: Oxford University Press, 1941).

Rita Hinden, *Plan for Africa* (London: Allen & Unwin, 1941).

Lord Hailey, *The Position of Colonies in the British Commonwealth of Nations* (London: Oxford University Press, 1941).

Four pamphlets on Africa representing the socialist and the liberal approach to the problem of Africa and the Africans.

W. M. Macmillan, *Democratise the Empire* (London: Kegan Paul, 1941).

A policy of colonial reform proposed by the well-known British expert.

JAWAHARLAL NEHRU, *The Unity of India* (London: Lindsay Drummond, 1941).
The collected writings of the Indian leader 1937 to 1940.

B. R. AMBEDKAR, *Thoughts on Pakistan* (Bombay: Thacker, 1941).
Pakistan, an independent federation of Islamic states in northern India, first suggested by the late poet Sir Mohammed Iqbal in 1930, was adopted by the Indian Moslem League in 1940. Dr. Ambedkar, the leader of India's Untouchables, favors the proposal.

J. CHINNA DURAI, *The Choice before India* (London: Jonathan Cape, 1941).
The author is friendly towards, and appreciative of, Great Britain.

SIR GEORGE SCHUSTER AND GUY WINT, *India and Democracy* (London: Macmillan, 1941).
Probably the best and most comprehensive recent study of India and of the tasks before India.

ARTHUR KOESTLER, *Scum of the Earth* (New York: Macmillan, 1941).
The book of a refugee on the fate of refugees, above all probably the best study of France at war and in disintegration. "The last grandiose effort to preserve the nineteenth-century idyll in the midst of an utterly unidyllic twentieth was the building of the Chinese Wall. For the same money and effort France could have built a modern, mechanized, and three-dimensional army. Why were the warnings of de Gaulle and Reynaud unheard, who from the early thirties onwards denounced the obsoleteness of the linear fortification system and advocated the system of highly motorized, mobile, relatively self-sufficient, and independent units, with an overwhelming air force?

The superficial answer is: because the arteriosclerotic French General Staff did not want to be bothered with any new-fangled ideas. But they could only get away with it because the Chinese Wall was indeed the projection of the nation's deep-felt wish to be left alone. De Gaulle's conception of an offensive army might have saved the peace by giving the Polish and Czech alliance a real meaning. But at that stage France no longer wanted to *save* the peace by any constructive effort; it wanted to be *left* in peace — and this psychological nuance made all the difference, and in fact sealed her fate."

YVES SIMON, *La Grande Crise de la République Française* (Montreal: Editions de l'Arbre, 1941).
Observations on the background of the French disaster, by a French Catholic philosopher. Important and penetrating.

"JACQUES," *A French Soldier Speaks* (London: Constable, 1941).
The meditations of a wounded French soldier who was evacuated from Dunkirk, and has since died in an English hospital. Translated by Helen Waddell. "To any reflective mind it is evident that the Revolution of 1793 had a moral consequence of which not the least profound was the cleavage of the country into two hostile camps. These major divisions split into various sub-divisions, but actually any one of these can still be referred to one or the other of the two main categories." "The real guilt lies at the door of the natural élite of the nation, whose hatred of democracy led them to betray their natural duty of leadership, and so left the field open to adventurers."

ALEXANDER WERTH, *Les Derniers Jours de Paris* (London: Hamish Hamilton, 1941).
Three preceding books by Werth, *France in Ferment, Which Way France?* and *France and Munich,* are the

most detailed story of France and the way to the abyss, 1933 to 1939.

ELIE J. BOIS, *Truth on the Tragedy of France* (London: Hodder & Stoughton, 1940).

On the background and the personalities of the breakdown of France by a French newspaper editor.

LOUIS LEVY, *Vérités sur la France* (Penguin Books, 1941).

The reasons for the downfall of France as seen by a French socialist.

JACQUES MARITAIN, *A travers le Désastre* (New York: Éditions de la Maison Française, 1941).

Probably the best non-political book on the breakdown of France by the well-known Catholic philosopher. "La détermination du général de Gaulle a soulagé bien des consciences; dans un moment de débâcle politique générale il s'est comporté en homme; son action peut devenir un facteur considérable dans les événements."

PHILIPPE BARRÈS, *Charles de Gaulle* (New York: Doubleday, Doran, 1941).

The author of the book is a well-known journalist of the French Right, the son of the famous French nationalist writer.

D. A. BINCHY, *Church and State in Fascist Italy* (London: Oxford University Press, 1941).

An excellent and fair book by a Catholic professor of legal history in Dublin who believes in the incompatibility of Fascism and Catholicism. A detailed and well-documented history of Italy from 1929 to 1939 and of Pius XI and Mussolini. See the review by Count Carlo Sforza in *Commonweal*, March 20, 1942.

"PENTAD," *The Remaking of Italy* (Penguin Books, 1941).

Five chapters on the history of Italy and her present

plight and her future by four Italians and one Englishman.

Sir John Maynard, *Russia in Flux* (London: Gollancz,
1941).
A penetrating study on Russia, old and new.

Arthur Koestler, *Darkness at Noon* (New York: Macmillan, 1941).
A psychological explanation of Communist attitudes
and of the famous Moscow trials in the form of a
novel written by a former communist.

Victor Gollancz, *Russia and Ourselves* (London: Gollancz, 1941).
Written by an English socialist after June 22, 1941.
It should be read in conjunction with the very important previous book by Victor Gollancz, John Strachey,
and George Orwell, *The Betrayal of the Left*, an ex-
amination and refutation of Communist policy from
October 1939 to January 1941 with an epilogue on
political morality (London: Gollancz, 1941).

Maurice Dobb, *Soviet Economy and the War* (London:
Routledge, 1941).
A careful analysis of the economic resources of the
Soviet Union.

G. D. H. Cole, *Europe, Russia and the Future* (London:
Gollancz, 1941).
A pamphlet written by a democratic socialist in sym-
pathy with the Soviet Union.

Joseph E. Davies, *Mission to Moscow* (New York: Simon
& Schuster, 1941).
Russia in 1936 to 1941 as viewed by an unprejudiced
American diplomat.

Walter Duranty, *The Kremlin and the People* (New
York: Reynal & Hitchcock, 1941).
The Russian development, as seen by an American

journalist very long acquainted with Russia, from the end of 1934 to 1941.

MAURICE HINDUS, *Hitler Cannot Conquer Russia* (New York: Doubleday, Doran, 1941).

"To depict the Russian earth and Russian humanity as they are today and the forces within them that make it impossible for a foreign invader to subjugate them."

MICHAEL MACALPIN, *Russia Fights* (London: Lawrence & Wishart, 1941).

A communist explains why the Germans failed in Russia. It was a people's war with complete unity behind the government, no fifth column, people's full confidence in the Red Army, every civilian ready not only to stay put but to fight, the absence of interests that hoped to share control of their property with the invader rather than destroy it, war material produced for defense and not profit, home front as well organized as the battle front.

J. T. MURPHY, *Russia on the March* (London: Bodley Head, 1941).

The author is a Marxist in sympathy with the Soviet Union.

STANTON LAUTENSCHLAGER, *Far West in China* (New York: Friendship Press, 1941).

Report of an American missionary who has been in China since 1920, about his visit to Communist China in the fall of 1940: ". . . unprecedented progress which has taken place in China's great Free West during the war years. Much of this progress is definitely related to Christianity. In the communist headquarters I found a new friendliness to Christianity and a new freedom for preaching."

KIM SAN AND NYM WALES, *Song of Ariran* (New York: John Day, 1941).

The life story of a Korean revolutionary as told to Mrs. Edgar Snow.

SYNGMAN RHEE, *Japan Inside Out* (New York: Fleming H. Revell, 1941).

The story of Japanese domination of Korea, by the President of the Korean National Government, and a warning, not heeded, to America.

INDEX